Christian Forgiveness

Christian Forgiveness

A New Understanding

DONALD ROSS ALGEO

WIPF & STOCK · Eugene, Oregon

CHRISTIAN FORGIVENESS
A New Understanding

Wipf & Stock
An Imprint of Wipf and Stock Publishers
199 W. 8th Ave., Suite 3
Eugene, OR 97401

www.wipfandstock.com

PAPERBACK ISBN: 979-8-3852-7513-7
HARDCOVER ISBN: 979-8-3852-7514-4
EBOOK ISBN: 979-8-3852-7515-1

VERSION NUMBER 04/03/26

This book is dedicated to my wife.

Contents

Acknowledgments

I WOULD LIKE TO express my appreciation to my friend, Marcy Downey, who proofread the original manuscript and provided a number of helpful suggestions.

Introduction

The practice of forgiveness is the central subject of Jesus Christ's instruction. According to his instruction, forgiveness supplies both the basis for personal salvation and sanctification, and also the singular tool God has provided for the accomplishment of his purposes for humanity.

In modern religious literature, forgiveness is treated largely as a psychotherapeutic tool, as a way through which personal disquiet and suffering may be remedied and interpersonal discord may occasionally be harmonized. Typically, real-life illustrations are offered of the beneficial psychological effects on individuals—benefits often bordering on miraculous—once they extend forgiveness to someone towards whom they have long harbored a hardened heart. And at the conclusion of these uplifting stories, the author claims to have demonstrated the meaning and truth of Christ's advocacy of the power and importance of forgiveness.

The background assumption of this body of literature is that Christ's principal concern is the emotional health of the individual, where *emotional* and *spiritual* are treated as synonymous. And so when examples are given of people achieving an inner peace after having practiced forgiveness, we are thought to have arrived at an understanding of why Jesus thought and spoke of it as the human practice of central and utmost divine importance, and manifested it to his dying moments.

But Jesus came to teach us things much deeper than we might learn from a competent psychotherapist. As useful as these books might be in pastoral counseling and pulpit encouragement, they only skim the surface of our Lord's full instruction about Christian forgiveness.

That instruction is the subject of this book.

* * * * *

In the natural social world, the world in which we are all born and raised, the social world that apportions rewards and punishments according to its own human sensibilities and moral intuitions, the virtue of forgiveness plays a decidedly secondary role compared to those of *fairness* and *justice*. Despite its antiquity and amendment by Christ, "eye for eye, tooth for tooth" remains even today the pragmatic moral rule we at least profess to adhere to in public life, and, if we are honest, almost always—at a minimum—do in practice adhere to in our private moral judgment.

And in the everyday world in which we conduct our practical lives, that is a sensible rule to live by: it provides a gratifying moral approbation to the systems of social and judicial administration that have established themselves on its foundation. That is why everyone feels morally satisfied when the bad guy gets his comeuppance. That is why proportionate retaliation, whether personal or civil or national, feels not only good but *right*, provided we believe ourselves or our community to have been wronged.

But in the Christian life, the landmarks have shifted from where they are in the natural life. The rules have changed. What applies here does not apply there, and vice versa. We need a guide for this new life, and by God's grace we have one in Christ. And what our guide teaches us is this: for Christians, for his committed followers, forgiveness is foundational for everything else, both on a personal spiritual level and in the accomplishment of God's larger purpose of human reconciliation.

The extended argument of this book is offered to corroborate these claims. We will proceed in three stages. In the first, we will discuss human forgiveness in general: what it is and what it isn't;

the roles it can play in human affairs; and the methods for and difficulties of its accomplishment.

With that conceptual framework in hand, we will then, in Part 2, be equipped to provide an understanding of the nature and operation of divine forgiveness. It must be emphasized for this stage that ours is a philosophic investigation of rational inquiry, not revelation, and we are well aware of the humility incumbent on those bringing merely human agency to issues of divine reality. Those very powers of rational thought, though, are themselves God-given, and meant to be utilized in seeking to know God. Their employment, therefore, in our present project, will be in accord with God's revealed intention, and by that harmony alone, may with God's blessing provide some insight, however incomplete, into the truth.

And finally, after analyzing the nature of human forgiveness in general, and using what we learn there to gain some understanding of divine forgiveness, we will move on to the extended study of Christian forgiveness in particular, of human forgiveness practiced by Christians.

What we will learn there is that such forgiveness exercises an authority, a privilege, and a responsibility unique to followers of Christ. We will learn that the exercise of that privileged authority in the practice of Christian forgiveness is the method God has ordained for spreading the life of the gospel—God's own nature—throughout rational creation. We will learn that the committed and disciplined practice of forgiveness opens the way to the acquisition and growth of all the spiritual fruits of the Christian life. And we will conclude with some practical advice on how to forgive.

These are large and momentous claims, and claims, like promises, are more easily made than fulfilled. The degree to which that fulfillment is accomplished in what follows is for the reader to decide. From those readers who are sincerely interested in the outcome of such an investigation, only two things are asked: first, their patience in following the argument in order through its stages, and especially through Part 1, which may seem overly mundane in its concerns and illustrations. And second, their forgiveness—Christian or otherwise—for the book's shortcomings, all of which derive from the author's many other human faults, but none from his lack of sincerity or desire to please and honor the author of our lives.

Part 1

Human Forgiveness

1

The Basics of Forgiveness

The notion of forgiveness finds its origin in the world of finance, and refers to the dismissal of monetary obligations, or debts. From there, it has been applied in a wide variety of contexts, including those of central concern in this book: the roles it plays in the divine plans for salvation. But the central logic of the financial relationship remains intact, however the notion of debt might have been expanded to include things other than money.

It will be a good starting place, therefore, to take a closer look at the core notion of forgiveness. That will give us the vocabulary and conceptual framework to advance our investigation into the matters of eternity.

* * * * *

Let us begin with a simple illustration of forgiveness in everyday life. Suppose I am driving home one dark and snowy night, and in a moment of distraction I turn into my neighbor's driveway instead of my own. Realizing my mistake, I hit the brakes, but the driveway is slick with snow and I skid forward and run into the back of her parked car.

Mortified, I climb out of my car just as my neighbor, having heard the noise, comes out her front door to see what happened. Together we survey the damage. Fortunately it is not very serious.

Her rear and my front bumper have matching dents, but the cost of the repairs will almost certainly not even rise above the level of our insurance deductibles: maybe a few hundred dollars each.

Still and all, since the accident was clearly and indisputably my fault, I immediately experience myself under a financial obligation to cover the cost of the repair to her car. However upset I might be with myself, however many potential excuses are running through my mind about the snowy weather and the obscured street light, whatever mitigating circumstances I can come up with to relieve my sense of moral guilt, the facts of the matter are so plain that there is no way to dispute my full and unqualified financial obligation to reimburse my neighbor for whatever it will cost to have her bumper repaired, or to directly pay for it myself.

But now suppose that my neighbor realizes that at this particular moment in time my circumstances are so financially straitened that even the few hundred dollars it will take to repair her bumper would impose a very difficult burden on me. And being the exceptionally decent person she is, she turns to me and says something along the following lines:

"Hey, listen, neighbor. I know this is about the last thing you need right now, so let's just pretend this didn't happen. Don't worry about my bumper. Come on inside and have a cranberry muffin, hot out of the oven!"

Wouldn't we all wish for neighbors like that! Figuratively speaking, when I ran into her car, I created an IOU, and her reaction amounted to tearing up the IOU and tossing it in the air, to blow away into the snowy night. And then offering me a muffin!

Here we have a small but perfect illustration of forgiveness in its purest original meaning. I have incurred a financial obligation—a debt—of the simplest, most straightforward, most unambiguous variety. I am fully aware of it, I admit it and the justice of it, I recognize my full responsibility for it. I am indebted to her, and until such time as I cover the cost of repairing her bumper, I will remain in her debt. It is like a burden which I must now carry, day and night, until I pay someone to take it off my shoulders.

But then my neighbor spoke her words of forgiveness, and immediately, with no effort on my part, my obligation disappears. The burden has been, as if by magic, lifted from my shoulders, without my having to pay anyone. One moment it is there, like a weight pressing down on me. The next moment, it is gone, and I am again as financially unencumbered as I had been before I made the fateful wrong turn into her driveway.

I have been forgiven.

So my debt is forgiven. But now we come to the important point, the point that must be fully understood in our simple little illustration in order eventually to appreciate why it is and how it is that forgiveness lies at the very heart of Christ's revelation. Here it is:

Although the debt is forgiven, the cost of repairing the bumper remains.

Somebody—in this case my generous neighbor—will have to take money from her own bank account and give it to the garage for repairs. Staying with our image, the burden I was carrying has not just magically dissolved, as if tapped by a fairy wand. What my neighbor has done, in effect, is to lift the burden from my shoulders and place it on her own. Her act of forgiveness has not eliminated the cost of my misadventure into her driveway—it has simply transferred the cost to herself.

In fact, thinking of debts as weights makes this very easy to visualize. When I borrow money, I may be thought of as accepting a weight or a burden, which is only reduced or removed to the degree I repay the money. If I don't repay the money, I continue to carry the burden.

In this image, someone forgiving me is taking the burden off of my shoulders. But it is of vital importance to note that, after taking if from me, she does not have the option of simply tossing it away on the side of the road. Once she has assumed the burden, she is now in the same condition I was: she will have to pay someone to take the burden off her. Forgiving someone's financial debt is *assuming* that person's financial burden.

And what is true of our simple illustration is true of financial forgiveness of any size or scope. If I borrow a thousand dollars from you and am unable to repay you, and if you forgive me my debt, what you are doing is bearing the loss of the thousand dollars yourself; you are absorbing the financial harm. If a municipality defaults on a bond and the citizen forgives—rather than sues—the local government, the citizen is assuming the burden of the financial loss. And so on.

The essential point is that a debt does not disappear when forgiven, like scraps of an IOU blowing off into the night. The weight of the debt is simply shifted from one party to the other.

Another way of expressing this is to say that the act of financial forgiveness is transactional: it amounts to a transaction in which the creditor takes *ownership* of the debt. In our example, the cost of repairing the damaged vehicle now *belongs* to my neighbor: it is no longer my debt—it is hers. She owns it now; it is now her responsibility to deal with as she chooses. For all intents and purposes, she is now financially related to the damage as if she had caused it herself. In this imagery, her forgiveness is like a writ of sale for a piece of property: her payment consists in the forgiveness, and the property consists of the damage. I now possess her forgiveness; she now possesses my responsibility for the accident. A transaction has taken place.

Because we tend to think of transactions in terms of an exchange of material possessions—money for property, for example—this may seem to be an unusual way of thinking about forgiveness; but there are in fact many transactions involving things other than physical goods for other physical goods. When I give you my word that I will take care of your house while you are on vacation, you now have my word, and I have the responsibility of safekeeping your house. When I attend to your instruction, you now have my attention, and I have your guidance. And so on.

Because we are accustomed to think of forgiveness mainly from the recipient's point of view, this seems at first like a strange, almost inverted way of thinking about forgiveness. We tend to think of it simply as a benefit, rather than an exchange, as a gift rather than what it really is: a purchase.

* * * * *

Returning to our simple illustration, there are several other points we must clarify at the outset.

The first is that financial forgiveness can be more or less complete. Suppose my neighbor, on surveying the damage and recollecting my pinched circumstances, had said something along the following lines:

"Hey, listen, neighbor. I know times are tough for you these days and I wish I could just say let's forget the whole thing. But I'm a little pinched right now myself, what with my wedding coming up and all. I tell you what let's do. We'll split the repair cost fifty-fifty. Now come on inside and we'll drown our sorrow in fresh muffins."

She is still forgiving me, but now her forgiveness is only partial: she will assume half the burden, take half the weight off my shoulders, absorb half the financial harm occasioned by my unfortunate turn into her driveway. Still an act of kindness, to be sure; just not quite so generous an act. And she still offered me a muffin!

Another thing we must be clear about is that there is one and only one person who can forgive me, and that is my neighbor, the one who owns the car, the one I have financially harmed. Other sorts of things might happen that would resolve our situation without my paying for the repair. Another neighbor, for example, having heard the crash, might come running from across the street and offer to repair the bumper for no charge. But that would not be forgiveness; that would be removing the need for forgiveness, an act of generosity of a different variety from forgiveness. The neighbor is bailing me and/or my neighbor out, but he is not forgiving either one of us.

Or while we are inside eating muffins, the woman's fiancé might drop by, hear the story of my mishap, and offer to pay for it himself, or to reimburse her whatever it will cost. Those will also be generous and kind acts, but they are not acts of forgiveness. The fiancé is covering her losses, but he is not forgiving her (or me).

The act of financial forgiveness is by definition a binary relationship between a debtor and a creditor, the one who owes and the one who is owed. Forgiveness can only happen between those two, and can only be accomplished by the creditor, the one who is owed.

It is also important to note that this same logic applies, regardless of the origin of the debt.

Suppose it is my son who is out driving my car on that blustery wintry night, and my son who mistakenly turns into her driveway and collides with her car. As his legally responsible parent, the debt accrued by this unfortunate accident still belongs to me. Should my neighbor choose to forgive the debt, it would be me she is forgiving, not my son.

The point is that debts can be acquired in a variety of ways, not all of which involve what we would consider moral culpability.

An even clearer example might involve citizens of a country ruled by tyrannical government, who are overtaxed into a state of impoverished subsistence. Cruel and wicked as the tax might be, it nonetheless establishes a creditor/debtor relationship; it imposes a financial burden on the citizens—although through no culpability of their own—a burden that can only be relieved, come tax time, by paying the tax, or through the government assuming its burden through forgiveness.

What we are learning is that the role of forgiveness stays the same—the transfer of financial burden—regardless of how the creditor/debtor relationship comes about.

* * * * *

There are still a number of things we must become clear about right at the beginning, and it will be helpful to stay with our simple illustration for a while yet.

The first of these is that financial forgiveness is an activity. It is not an emotion like fear or a feeling like a headache. Nor is it a condition of the person, like being aggravated or distraught or confused. The forgiveness lies in the action, not in the motivation for the action.

Suppose my neighbor harbors a grudge of long-standing against me: I do not maintain my lawn properly and my dog once bit her fiancé. Nonetheless, she has always been taught and tries to live her life in accordance with the dictum "To err is human, to forgive divine." Therefore, her smile in this scenario perhaps a strained grimace, she pronounces her words of forgiveness.

Despite her inner chagrin, the forgiveness is accomplished. The financial burden is shifted from me to her, whether she is feeling warm and generous about it, or resentful and angry. The forgiveness lies in the action on the stage, so to speak, and not in whatever might be happening behind the scenes (although needless to say, there will be no offer of muffins in this particular production!).

Or again, the bank manager who forgives my final installment of a loan repayment according to bank policy may be thinking about what she will order for lunch as she signs the release. No matter; I am forgiven. She may not even have any personal acquaintance with me, or for that matter even have any idea who I am. No matter; I am forgiven. She may in fact wish in her heart of hearts that the bank had no such policy of forgiving the final payment; she may regard the policy as ill considered, or unfair, or as a violation of the bank's fiduciary responsibilities to its shareholders. No matter. My loan is still forgiven, simply by the action of the pen in her hand.

The one constant in the various financial scenarios we are considering is the actual action whereby the burden to repay is shifted from the debtor to the creditor: the words spoken by my neighbor, the signature provided by the bank manager. All the rest simply gives us more information about the basic action of forgiveness, about its motives or context.

As an aside, we should mention here that having established this is not to deny that a person's behavior provides excellent reason for making inferences about the inner life of people, about the qualities of their personalities. Always allowing for the complexities and peculiarities of the interior life, for the possibilities of deceit or self-delusion, the woman whose social life exhibits a pattern of generosity may confidently be expected to harbor a tender heart. The man who hazards his own well-being for patriotic cause gives evidence of his dedication to his ideals. And the one whose public life is populated with acts of forgiveness is in all likelihood possessor of a native empathy. But these are probabilities, not certainties. The novelist's art is to explore these fascinating regions of the spirit, and we will ourselves return to the topic later.

Nor is it to deny that the quality of the inner life is of the utmost importance. The quality of that life is in fact central to Christ's instruction in the matter of forgiveness. "Unless you forgive from the heart" is the phrase he uses to provide the moral for the parable of the unmerciful servant (Matt 18:21–35), and he is obviously speaking there, not only about the basic act of forgiveness, but about the spiritual source of the act. The quality of mercy is not strained in the forgiveness Christ is seeking, but rather flows freely and naturally. And when we come to the full discussion of that instruction, this topic will in fact be one of our main concerns.

But to return to our main line of analysis, for now we are still laying the foundation for that larger discussion, and our current aim is to focus strictly on the act itself, rather than its motivations. And what we have discovered about the basic act of financial forgiveness is that, essentially, it is the transference of a financial burden from a debtor to a creditor by a willful action of the creditor.

Another way of putting this is that financial forgiveness names an accomplishment that can be verified by referencing a particular publicly observable action. It has that in common with many other accomplishments. Marrying someone is accomplished by an authorized individual signing a document. Winning a marathon is accomplished by being first across a line. Breaking the law is accomplished by an action in violation of an established statute.

Similarly, forgiving someone is accomplished by doing something that can be publicly verified, whether word or deed.

* * * * *

Another thing we must be clear about in this introductory examination is that for there to be financial forgiveness there must have been financial harm. Effectively beneficial acts offer no occasion for forgiveness. Suppose that instead of running into my neighbor's car, I had instead mowed her lawn. Here there is no opportunity for her financial forgiveness. If she, surveying my handiwork, were to say "I forgive you for this," I would have to assume that I had unwittingly somehow done her financial harm, perhaps by destroying the new species of grass she was growing, unbeknownst to me. Lacking any such discovery of hidden harm, there is simply nothing to forgive, and her words, if they are to have any meaning at all, must have been spoken facetiously.

Or consider again the action of my banker. Suppose I had already fully paid my loan, and it is only through a bookkeeping error that my account still shows an outstanding obligation. Here her act of affixing her signature to a bank document, however else it might be described, could not meaningfully be categorized as an act of forgiveness.

Financial forgiveness can only be accomplished in response to actual financial debt. In the absence of such debt, even if the formulae for extending forgiveness—certain customary words, for example—are invoked, they accomplish nothing in the way of actual forgiveness. They are like words of forgiveness spoken by one actor to another in a play, or the utterance of a fictional character in a novel. They are not examples of forgiveness; they are simply dialog in a fictional context.

* * * * *

So far we have learned that financial forgiveness, in its essence, is the transference of an actual financial burden from a debtor to a creditor, and that its accomplishment is a publicly observable action, not an emotion or state of mind.

The final point to be clear about is that it runs counter to justice.

Our language is replete with expressions that reflect how deep-seated the calculation of fairness is in our estimation of what should be done in cases where there is some conflict of interest. *Fair's fair*, we say. *He should pay; it's only right. He shouldn't get off scot-free here!*

When I ran into my neighbor's car, I think we would all agree that it is *right* that I be held accountable, that the cost of repairing her car *should* be my responsibility. Certainly if she had filed a police report and taken me to court, that would have been the court's finding. But beyond that, it just seems right, does it not? It is not just a matter of legality; it is a matter of morality; or perhaps we should say our laws, at least ideally, are passed to reflect our morality, our native sense of right and wrong. We may debate how the recognition of fairness becomes so ingrained in the human way of regarding things, but it is indisputably there. Even hardened criminals and sociopaths acknowledge it, as witness their moral indignation when they believe themselves to have been treated unfairly.

The significance of this might become clearer if we make a few changes to our illustration.

Suppose instead of a wintry night it was a clear and sunny afternoon. And suppose I am returning home from a bar where I have had too much to drink. And suppose I am having an animated and inebriated conversation with someone on my cell phone when I make the wrong turn into my neighbor's driveway and smash into my neighbor's car. She comes running from the house and finds me leaning drunkenly against my car, looking sheepishly guilty while from the cell phone still in my hand someone is yelling *What happened, man? What was that crash sound?*

My neighbor may still forgive me, but it will now be doubly hard. She must now not only bear the cost of repairing the bumper herself, but she must also act contrary to her own sense of justice, that fundamental moral point of view that we all share.

For many, both philosophers and ordinary people, the belief is that balancing the books somehow lies at the foundation of morality, of our estimation of what *should* be done, of the way things *should* work. Had my neighbor not been the naturally sweet and kind soul she is, she might very easily have reacted with righteous indignation to my careless driving. And notice that I did not just say *indignation*—I said *righteous* indignation. She would not just have been angry at me, but her anger would have been experienced by her as justified. *And not just by her.* Any unbiased spectators of the scene would have been of the same opinion. And had she under those conditions still chosen to forgive me, she would have been overriding her own sense of fairness.

Forgiveness then can involve not just a personal financial cost, but a violation of our fundamental ethical principle, the principle of fairness. It is exactly that calculation of fairness that forgiveness overrides.

And this is always the case with forgiveness, understood as an activity and not as an emotion. Where both parties behave strictly according to the calculations of justice and fairness, there is no opening for forgiveness. Justice and fairness are in essence calculative: a society of robots could be perfectly just. But forgiveness steps outside that calculation: that is why forgiveness could never evolve out of a society of purely calculative agents.

* * * * *

We will conclude this opening chapter by saying a few words about what we will now proceed to build on its foundation. We have learned that financial forgiveness always involves bearing one sort of burden, and the potential for bearing another. The first is the financial burden of a debt. The second is the psychological burden of acting contrary to one's own standard of justice.

Both of these factor into why forgiveness is sometimes hard, sometimes very hard, indeed.

Consider my friendly neighbor. The damage I did to her car was relatively minor: a bruised fender. But it need not have been minor. I might have struck her car so hard that it was completely destroyed. Now not just the bumper, but the entire car must be replaced!

She may still forgive me. But if she does, she is assuming a far larger burden, one which we can imagine would be very heavy to bear.

So that is one way in which financial forgiveness can be difficult. The other, as we have seen, may in many cases be even more burdensome. A gambling debt generally incurs less human sympathy than an accidentally dented bumper, less inclination to assume its cost, and correspondingly greater reluctance to forgive.

These are the reasons why it is often so hard to forgive in the mundane world of finance. And as we now move into the world of the spirit, we will find that the difficulties there are vastly deeper and greater, yet fundamentally of the same sort. And we will see how forgiveness is perhaps the hardest thing of all to do in the spiritual life.

But now that we have clarified our thinking, now that we have understood the underlying logic of forgiveness, we have the tools to begin our exploration of why and how forgiveness, in the far more important matters to which we now turn our attention, commands the central position in God's plan of salvation.

2

Forgiveness of Other Harms

In the preceding chapter, we arrived at an understanding of forgiveness according to which it, in essence, consists in bearing the burden of the harm done to oneself by someone else. Our understanding was based upon and derived from an examination of examples of financial harm, both because that variety of harm provides the prototype opportunity for forgiveness, and also because such cases offer a relatively simple quantification both of the harm and of its forgiveness. The cost of the harm done by me running into the back of my neighbor's car is easily and adequately represented by a monetary amount that can be ascertained by a call to a body repair shop.

As we move forward from those basic illustrations to the larger and, for our purposes, far more significant matters of forgiveness, the means of quantifying the harm done and the cost of forgiveness becomes much more complicated.

To begin again with a relatively simple example: if I willingly insult my neighbor to her face, I have probably done her harm, but there is no comparably simple way of measuring its degree or nature. While we may continue to speak of the emotional or psychological *cost* to her of my insult, it is clear that "cost" is now being used metaphorically rather than literally, as it was in the case of my damaging her bumper. There is no established medium of measurement available to quantify the harm done to her by my insult as there was to quantify the harm done to her bumper.

But the conceptual analysis of the situation remains unaffected by this complication. Should she choose to forgive me for insulting her, my neighbor's forgiveness of my insult still consists in her bearing the insult's cost to her, regardless of how that cost is to be reckoned. The debt to her which I have incurred is not a financial debt, but it is a debt nonetheless, and while the burden of debt which she metaphorically removes from me is no longer a financial burden, it is a burden nonetheless.

Put in the most general way, the financial forgiveness of a debtor by a creditor consists in the restoration by the creditor of the financial relationship that existed between the two prior to the harm. In our basic illustration, my neighbor's forgiveness of me accomplishes that restoration: she has and makes no further financial claim on me.

And in the same general sense, the accomplishment of forgiveness in cases of other kinds of harm consists in the restoration of the original human and social relationship *of the creditor towards the debtor* that existed prior to the harm. The effects of that forgiveness may manifest themselves in many ways on the part of the debtor, but whatever their nature might be is irrelevant to the forgiveness itself. Forgiveness is always and only the prerogative and bailiwick of the creditor.

These are the matters to which we will now turn.

* * * * *

Perhaps the best way to approach a full discussion of the forgiveness of nonfinancial harm is to hearken back to something we also discussed in chapter 1, namely, that forgiveness can be more or less complete.

In the case of financial harm, this observation is fairly straightforward. If I owe you a hundred dollars and you forgive fifty of the debt, your forgiveness was only partial—half, in fact—while you still retain a claim on me for the remaining fifty dollars. In such cases, it is easy to see and calculate what amounts to complete and what amounts to partial forgiveness.

In other kinds of harm, the calculation becomes more problematic. We have said that forgiveness in the case of such harm consists in the restoration by the one harmed of his or her original human and social relationship to the one who caused the harm. But how does that simple formula translate into the variables of real life?

When I insult my neighbor, the personal harm done to her may be slight or it may be overwhelming, depending on her own personality. We express those possibilities colloquially by saying that some people have thicker skin than others. An insult that might mortify my sensitive neighbor to the west may have little or no effect on my thicker-skinned neighbor to the east, and the "cost" of forgiveness on their separate parts will vary accordingly.

For my callous neighbor, the cost is minimal. Whatever his attitudes and feelings about me were before the insult, thus they remain largely unaffected after it. If his wife were to remind him of the insult, he might say something along these lines: "Oh that? I just laughed it off. What difference does it make to me what *he* thinks?"

Forgiveness, by such an individual, comes at little or even no cost. For him, the harm done was so slight as to be scarcely noticeable. As we noted in our earlier discussion, forgiveness presupposes harm, but we might now add that the difficulty of forgiveness is a function of the degree of experienced harm. My thick-skinned neighbor has experienced little or no harm, and therefore, for him, there is little, perhaps nothing, to forgive. My insult has affected him no more than a gnat flying by his ear. He is, in fact, someone who embodies the advice *to forgive and forget*, and the conjunction of those two in commonplace wisdom is no accident. To forgive completely, from the point of view of the forgiver, is indistinguishable from complete forgetfulness. From that point of view, it is literally *as if* the harmful act had never occurred.

Contrast that with my sensitive neighbor on the other side. My insult to her was experienced as a deadly blow rather than a gnat's unnoticed passage. Her ego is bruised, her self-image shaken, her faith and trust in humanity diminished. For her to recover her earlier feelings and attitudes towards me will be a formidable, perhaps nigh impossible, project. The human possibility of complete forgiveness in this case is vanishingly small.

And the human possibilities become more various and complicated as we move on to more poignant cases of harm. When a terrorist sets off a bomb in a crowded location, the single act of detonating the explosive device creates multiple possibilities for forgiveness, each of which will have its own character.

* * * * *

We have spoken above about the difficulty of measuring the degree and nature of nonfinancial harm, due to the variable and various sensibilities of those suffering such harm. What remains for us to discuss are some of the common elements of human nature that render forgiveness of such harm difficult, regardless of its experienced magnitude.

First and foremost is that same element that opposes the pursuit and accomplishment of any of the Christian virtues. I am referring of course to pride.

Pride is the elevation of oneself over another, and so the very first movement of forgiveness runs contrary to pride's impulse. When someone willfully harms you, that deliberate infliction of harm is typically an assertion of status; it is the other asserting an authority over you, whether it be an authority of strength or of social position or of moral superiority, or some combination of these. Pride's impulse is to defend or restore or even elevate one's own status, and the impulse is extraordinarily difficult to resist. Swallowing one's pride amounts to accepting the lowered position of status the willful harm has asserted.

That sounds very abstract, but we will all recognize its truth in everyday experience. A discourteous clerk in a clothing store wounds our pride because the social position of clerk is supposed to be deferential to the social position of customer. A husband's condescending criticism wounds the wife's pride as a coequal in the relationship. "Who do you think *you* are?" is the quintessential assertion of wounded pride in the arena of social relations.

And so the very first movement of forgiveness—the acceptance of harm—must contend with that natural human desire to reclaim status.

But the effort of will required to forgive requires even more than that, especially when we remember that forgiveness lies along a spectrum of completeness, from grudging and superficial at one end to full and complete at the other.

We are all aware of the enormous effort and vigilance and determination it takes to do good anonymously. Doing good itself is relatively easy: every hour of every day offers abundant opportunity. There are many people who fill their days with doing good things for others.

But what is psychologically very difficult for most people is to do good—especially good that comes at a significant cost to oneself—in the complete absence of any recognition.

This is, of course, not limited to altruistic behavior. It is almost a part of the definition of what it is to be human that we live our lives in the constant sense that others are paying attention to us, and the constant desire that they are admiring or at least forming a positive opinion of us, whether it be in athletics or art or politics or education or courting or just simple conversation. Even at the pathological extreme of complete narcissism, the supposed audience doesn't disappear; it is simply internalized and then projected.

Doing good for others—as in forgiveness—does not escape this net. We are all familiar with the phenomenon commonly called *humble bragging* or *false modesty*. Most of us are probably aware of it in ourselves. It amounts to presenting oneself to one's audience with the point of winning their approval or admiration while disguising that intention. It is a variety of vanity, and in social terms, relatively harmless, often even humorous.

But in spiritual terms, it can be deadly, because it is also a variety of hypocrisy, of feigned innocence. There is literally nothing against which Jesus warns us more strongly, even though, again, from the world's view, it seems relatively benign.

When you fast, do it cheerfully. When you pray, do it secretly. These are ways of saying that, above all things, your own good deeds must not be corrupted by any element of self-publicity, of seeking the admiration of others. To the extent they are, the *weight* of their goodness, in heaven's calculation, is diminished. *Beware of practicing your righteousness before other people in order to be seen by them.*

Forgiveness tests the limit of our obedience to that instruction. When someone has wrongly harmed you, even after you have mustered the determination to forgive that person there remains a well-nigh irresistible human desire that someone recognize your determination, that someone applaud your magnanimity, first and foremost, perhaps, the person you have determined to forgive.

In our illustration, my extraordinarily good neighbor, having forgiven me, immediately offers an invitation to come inside and have a muffin. What is she doing here? She is restoring our prior relationship as neighbors by deflecting all attention from the act of kindness she has just shown towards me. She is deflecting my attention away from my feelings of guilt and relief, even of gratitude. What she is doing in offering me a muffin is in some respects even greater than the act of generosity itself: having shouldered my burden, she is now healing me.

When forgiving someone for harm done to oneself, the final and often most important element is that it be accomplished, so to say, anonymously. In practical terms, that means behaving towards the person in question, insofar as possible, as if the harm had never occurred.

That, in fact, is what forgiveness is, spiritually speaking. It is shouldering the burden of the damage done to oneself, while healing whatever damage the other might have suffered. The damage and pain themselves that result from spiritual wickedness and carelessness cannot be undone. They are eternal. Forgiveness does not remove them; nothing can do that. What forgiveness does is bring them to a conclusion, soothe them with love's ointment, and leave them behind.

The world offers many ways of dealing with evil individuals, but forgiveness is God's only method of dealing with the evil within them.

And as if that were not enough human difficulty for forgiveness to overcome, there is yet one more factor. We swallow our pride to forgive, we struggle with our vanity in forgiving fully, and finally, we must tolerate the shame that is often involved.

Much of the harm we suffer is public harm in the sense that others besides our direct antagonist may very well be aware of it, and aware of our response. Being slapped on one cheek and turning the other will often occur in a social context, and social contexts consist of individuals with their own perspective on one's reaction. Someone witnessing you striking me on the cheek and me not responding in kind is very apt to align his or her perspective with that of the person who struck me, is very apt to see my antagonist's assertion of status over me as legitimate.

Thus, to turn the other cheek—to forgive—is not only to swallow my pride, but also to accept the embarrassment and shame of acquiescing to a lowered status in the opinion of onlookers.

While, phrased that way, it sounds awfully abstract and pedantic, ordinary experience will again offer us many examples we can identify with. A man who refuses to defend himself against attack when it is in his power to do so is typically not regarded as a saint, but as a coward or worse. A woman who submits without resistance to her husband's bullying is pitied, not applauded. Thus, to the difficulties posed by pride and vanity, we must add social ignominy to the burden forgiveness asks us to bear.

Reflection on these complexities makes it clear that virtually all opportunities for forgiveness of nonfinancial harm will fall somewhere along a continuum in terms of their difficulty, with complete forgiveness being rare, perhaps even representing an impossible ideal, its nearest human approach being when nothing remains of the event in the forgiver's spirit other than, as it were, a mental notation, having no further effect on the forgiver than the reflection of a cloud on a lake does on the waters below its surface.

Human nature with its many limitations will for these reasons condemn most sincere attempts at forgiveness to fall somewhere short of that ideal. Complete forgiveness of my insult by my extremely sensitive neighbor consists in her once again feeling and acting towards me in the same ways she did prior to the emotional harm I inflicted on her, as if she had literally forgotten the insult. But my neighbor's feelings and attitudes and memories are not easily manipulated. They are part of her psychic reality rather than her legal or moral circumstances. There is nothing she can *do* that thereby immediately alters her psychic condition the way uttering a few words effectively alters her financial situation.

And this is true of most varieties of personal harm suffered from the willful misbehavior of others. When one has been emotionally damaged, the pain lingers and the wound leaves its mark in analogy to physical abuse. We are not computers (yet!), and we don't have buttons to push or switches to engage that will restore us to an earlier condition.

Or to put it straightforwardly, forgiveness can be hard, sometimes very hard indeed, complete forgiveness perhaps even humanly impossible in most cases. But this will come as no surprise to those familiar with themselves and their fellow human beings. Few of us, if we are being honest, can point to many examples in our own histories where emotional damage done to us by the intentional behavior of someone else has left no lingering trace on the internal economy of our spirits. Complete forgiveness in most cases will always remain an ideal, a condition which, should we embark on its achievement, will normally remain a destination, a distant shore towards which we are traveling rather than a conquest on which we can now plant our flag.

But having acknowledged the ways in which human nature complicates the task of complete forgiveness, we are still warranted in saying that, however difficult its achievement, complete forgiveness amounts to the return of the forgiver to the attitudes and behavior towards the subject of forgiveness that obtained prior to the experienced harm, whatever its magnitude and nature. And that is all we need to continue our investigation, and to narrow its focus from forgiveness in general to Christian forgiveness in particular.

* * * * *

In these opening chapters, our concern has been simply to arrive at an understanding of what forgiveness is, without entering into the question of how it is to be accomplished. Since our determination that forgiveness of most harms, in essence, consists of a spiritual (psychological, emotional, attitudinal) evolution or journey, the cautionary remarks immediately above may leave the reader with some concern about its apparent difficulty.

For the Christian, those concerns are certainly justified in light of the many evidences in Scripture that forgiveness of others lies at the very heart of the obedient Christian life. "Blessed are the merciful" . . . "turn the other cheek" . . . "love your enemy"; these and many other elements of our Lord's instruction clearly posit forgiveness at the center of that life, and it therefore behooves us to investigate how to go about it. That will, in fact, be the investigation that concludes this treatise. But for now, we will simply make two observations.

The first is that we must never let the perfect be the enemy of the good. Complete forgiveness shares with perfection in any of the virtues the role of an ideal, towards which we are enjoined to strive, rather than of an object of guaranteed success.

That perfect virtue may, for now, be the province of divinity rather than humanity is suggested in many places in Scripture, perhaps nowhere more clearly than in the inspired word of Jeremiah, writing of our own topic, forgiveness:

> But this is the covenant that I will make with the house of Israel after those days, declares the LORD: I will put my law within them, and I will write it on their hearts. And I will be their God, and they shall be my people. And no longer shall each one teach his neighbor and each his brother, saying, "Know the LORD," for they shall all

> know me, from the least of them to the greatest, declares the LORD. For I will forgive their iniquity, and I will remember their sin no more. (Jer 31:33–34)

The second is that such perfection, even if for now reserved for divinity, is nonetheless enjoined upon us by our Lord: "You therefore must be perfect, as your heavenly Father is perfect" (Matt 5:48). However exactly that challenging injunction is to be construed, we must allow that, at the very least, it asks of us a serious attempt to model our lives after that of the example set for us by our Lord and Savior, and promises divine approbation of our attempt.

Needless to say, the Christian life is not one of perfection; but it is the life that sets its compass by the lodestar of Christ's perfection, and journeys accordingly. What better thought to conclude our investigation of human forgiveness, and move forward to an investigation of its divine counterpart?

Part 2

Divine Forgiveness

3

The Spiritual Dimension

It is not the concern of this present work to prove the existence of the divine dimension, or more simply, to prove the existence of God. Everything we have to offer from this point on will simply assume God's existence; more specifically, we will assume the existence of the God revealed by Christian Scripture to pious Christian reflection. Our object henceforward is to describe the place and function of forgiveness in reality as reality is understood and believed in by traditional Christianity. Should *per impossible* those beliefs be mistaken, then what follows will have only academic interest to students of the Christian religion. But to those invested existentially in the truth of Christianity, in the instruction and guidance and promises it provides, an understanding of divine forgiveness is the necessary preliminary to an appreciation of the nature, importance, and role of forgiveness in the individual and corporate Christian life.

Let us then proceed to that investigation.

* * * * *

In part 1, we limited our discussion of forgiveness to the purely human point of view. Virtually everything we have said about it would still be true if there were no God, or if Jesus had not revealed to us the ways of God's kingdom. The reality and significance of forgiveness would be exhausted by discovering its human application to situations in which someone has incurred harm as a consequence of the behavior of someone else.

If we were merely material beings, on our own in the universe with only other material beings; if there were no living relationships beyond those we share with others like ourselves; if the consequences of our harmful behavior reached no farther than the human recipients of that behavior . . . if all these things were true, then the considerations we have presented in part 1 would be substantially all there is to say about the concept of forgiveness.

Of course, forgiveness might still have a valuable role to play in a godless universe, and we might even there talk about the desirability of this particular method of conflict resolution, in comparison with its absence. We might argue for its benefits both to society in general and to the forgiver in particular. And in fact, it is worth taking a few moments here to talk about each of these two possible benefits, because they will continue to play their parts in the richer spirit-filled universe we do in fact live in, and which provides the setting for our deeper analysis of Christian forgiveness.

So, to take the former sort of benefit, we might discuss the comparative societal preferability of forgiveness to other methods of resolution, to retributive justice, for example. We might argue that a society in which forgiveness is at least occasionally operative among its members results in a society of greater stability and harmony than a society in which retribution, whether personal or delegated, is the sole method of dealing with harm.

In making this case, we would no doubt point both to the tendency of human nature to overreact to suffered harm, and to the difficulty for delegated societal agency of accurately measuring the harm suffered by its members.

The Hatfield and McCoy saga would provide a powerful illustration of the tendency of human nature to overreact to personal harm, and of the ever-spiraling and spreading consequent social instability that can result from the unchecked operation of the nigh-universal human impulse to seek retribution. Left to its own carnal devices, the dynamics of human nature tend all too readily to the multiplication of harm, rather than its limitation. Thomas Hobbes famously summarized the societal outcome of individuals left to their own natural devices for resolving conflict as "solitary, poor, nasty, brutish, and short."

Hobbes, of course, offered this as a rationale for allowing to social governance the authority for resolving such conflict, and we will return to that in a moment. But for now, we are simply considering what one might argue in favor of forgiveness as a socially desirable mechanism for resolving conflict among its members. A society in which the growth of harm is, occasionally at least, curtailed by personal forgiveness would, according to this argument, be preferable to one in which the proliferation of that harm is left unchecked. And this would surely be a powerful argument.

And as for delegating the responsibility for satisfactory retributive justice to governmental authority—*a la* Hobbes—the difficulties here are also considerable, with the possibilities for miscarriages of justice rivaling and perhaps surpassing those attending the Hatfield-McCoy difficulty.

Governmental authority, after all, amounts to nothing other than the authority of people occupying certain social stations, and those peoples' determinations can and almost certainly will be influenced to some degree by the elements of their own personalities: boredom, hastiness, outrage, professional aspirations, and so on. Where a Hatfield's disproportionate response might result from the seductive allure of vengeance, the magistrate's might equally err through moral distaste or political ambition, or by any of the other myriad natural human proclivities that flesh is heir to.

And this does not even touch on the deeper and more intractable difficulties of accurately measuring the harm experienced by someone else. To return to one of our earlier examples, a magistrate charged with meting out punishment for a casual insult, lacking God's knowledge of the human heart, can only hazard a guess at the depth and extent of the actual emotional harm suffered from the insult—mere human judgment could never accurately gauge the debt due this particular sufferer.

Given these difficulties, an advocate for forgiveness—still speaking of a purely material world—might powerfully argue that a society in which personal forgiveness has a substantial part to play in the resolution of personal harm would be a more efficient and even a fairer society than one in which all such resolution was left in the hands of "blind" administrative justice.

So, even if we were to restrict our investigation to a godless world, the case for forgiveness might be powerfully and effectively argued by pointing out the comparative communal benefits accruing to societies that grant personal forgiveness a significant role to play in the resolution of interpersonal harm over societies in which it is lacking. Even Hobbes might be persuaded by such arguments.

And again, still setting religious considerations aside and speaking of a purely secular world, considerations might be advanced concerning the individual therapeutic benefits that often accrue to those who practice forgiveness of personal harm. Psychological studies are replete with such illustrations. When viewed through the prism of *emotional recovery* or *psychic health*, human life affords many examples in which a grievance long harbored, once forgiven, is experienced by the sufferer as a release into an emotionally and psychically better place.

(To get ahead of ourselves for a moment, most books about Christian forgiveness in the current era restrict their advocacy to illustrating—through anecdote and case histories—personal psychological benefits of this sort. And while that is all well and good, and certainly does reflect many cases of lived Christian biography, the secular writer can point to similar benefits to non-Christians of the practice of forgiveness. Such Christian books, in other words, are generally focused on the personal benefits of forgiveness in general, and not of Christian forgiveness in particular, all the while omitting discussion of the spiritually precedent questions of its special nature, its special privilege, and its special responsibility—that is, of the topics of this present volume. Once we have completed our investigation of those foundational matters, we will return to the topic of the special spiritual benefits of Christian forgiveness in the final chapter of this book.)

And so, to summarize, the activity of forgiveness, as we have analyzed it earlier, has much to recommend it, even outside the context of Christian truth, even in a world containing no spiritual order beyond that of rational material beings.

But we do not live in such a universe. Ours is a God-created universe in which we stand in a relationship to our creator God, the nature of which has been fully revealed by Jesus Christ.

And if we accept that as a starting point, and then turn again to the activity of forgiveness, what we will find is that forgiveness acquires dimensions and functions in addition to those we have discussed so far, and an importance both to ourselves and to God that is impossible to exaggerate. Indeed, as we shall see, Christian forgiveness—forgiveness practiced by Christians—is the central and foundational element in personal salvation as well as the God-ordained means of bringing about the reconciliation of humanity to himself.

In a word, it is the key to the kingdom of God.

4
Harming God

In the worldly way of thinking, if I harm someone and that person forgives me, that is the end of the matter. We saw earlier how rare and difficult complete forgiveness is, but this simple fact about forgiveness remains unaffected by that scarcity. Whether partial or complete, the act of forgiveness, in a purely material world, is strictly a relationship between two individuals: the one harmed and the one doing the harm. The forgiveness that takes place between them, no matter its degree, directly alters the relationship between those two and those two only. And if there were no God, that would indeed be the end of the matter. But the reality of God means, among many other things, that the harm I do in the worldly realm has a counterpart harm in the spiritual realm.

Consider this remarkable fact, well attested to in the Gospel accounts: Jesus forgave strangers for their sins. Why is that remarkable? Because given what we have learned heretofore, such forgiveness is impossible.

Why is it impossible?

Because they were strangers.

The two most straightforward examples offered us by the Gospel writers are the paralyzed man described in Mark 2:1–12 (see also Matt 9:1–8; Luke 5:17–26), and the woman "of the city" about whom we read in Luke 7:36–50.

In Mark's recounting of the former case, we find four men carrying their paralyzed friend on a pallet. They are seeking to bring him face-to-face with Jesus for his miraculous healing, but they find their efforts frustrated by the crowds blocking the way into the house in which Jesus is holding forth. Improvising on the spot, they carry their friend by an external stairway up a level, and then proceed to remove some of the roofing material and lower their friend into the crowded room below. On seeing their faith, Mark tells us, Jesus informs the paralyzed man that his sins are forgiven. Here is the passage in question:

> And when he returned to Capernaum after some days, it was reported that he was at home. And many were gathered together, so that there was no more room, not even at the door. And he was preaching the word to them. And they came, bringing to him a paralytic carried by four men. And when they could not get near him because of the crowd, they removed the roof above him, and when they had made an opening, they let down the bed on which the paralytic lay. And when Jesus saw their faith, he said to the paralytic, "Son, your sins are forgiven." (Mark 2:1–5)

And the same announcement by Jesus is made, according to Luke, in the home of Simon, a Pharisee who has invited Jesus to dine with him. A woman described by Luke as "a sinner" is also there, and at a certain moment, while comparing the effusive welcome provided him by the woman to the lukewarm reception of the host himself, Jesus informs the woman, in the same simple and direct way he informs the paralyzed man, that her sins are forgiven.

> Then turning toward the woman he said to Simon, "Do you see this woman? I entered your house; you gave me no water for my feet, but she has wet my feet with her tears and wiped them with her hair. You gave me no kiss, but from the time I came in she has not ceased to kiss my feet. You did not anoint my head with oil, but she has anointed my feet with ointment. Therefore I tell you, her sins, which are many, are forgiven—for she loved much.

> But he who is forgiven little, loves little." And he said to her, "Your sins are forgiven." (Luke 7:44–48)

Those present on both occasions marvel at his words; in the first example, some "teachers of the law" are religiously scandalized, believing only God could offer such forgiveness; in the latter example, Simon the Pharisee surmises that Jesus must not be aware of the appalling nature of the woman's sins.

And we also marvel at his words, but for a much different reason. Given what we have discovered about the logic of forgiveness, the actions of Jesus were not simply presumptuous (the Pharisees' evaluation) nor a product of ignorance (Simon's evaluation). Based on what we have learned, such forgiveness was conceptually impossible, and the words offering it on both occasions, therefore, simply meaningless.

Why? Because in neither case had Jesus been the recipient of any harm from the object of his proffered forgiveness.

Suppose a man you do not recognize walks up to you on the street and says, in seeming seriousness, "I forgive you." What is your reaction?

You might, of course, simply brush him aside and continue unaffected on your way. But assuming an element of sympathetic conscience entering into your reaction, its first stage would be for you to cast about in your mind for some occasion or previous acquaintance on which you had done something to harm this man. If you now remember such an occasion, the perplexity is resolved. Whatever subsequent elements there might be in your reaction, at least the man's words addressed to you now make sense.

Or if you cannot in the surprise of the moment bring anything to mind, you might even ask the man to jar your memory, to remind you of when you had met before, and what you had done to warrant his words. And if he does in fact describe such an incident, then again, whether you now remember it or whether you still have no such recollection, at least the man's words make sense to you. Your memory might be unreliable, or the man might have mistaken you for someone else, or, at the extreme, he might be delusional; but he is still making sense; he is still using words in conformity to the rules of semantics you both share.

But suppose the man replies to your inquiry that he has never met you before. "Then what have I ever done to you?" you exclaim, still seeking for meaning in his words. "Perhaps I've hurt a member of your family, or of someone else you care about?"

"Nothing," he says. "You have never hurt me or anyone I know or even anyone I know about."

You are now flummoxed. You have now pursued the investigation as far as it can go, and you must conclude that the man is unaware of the meaning of his own words, either through mental unbalance, or perhaps because he is a foreigner who has chosen the wrong word to express whatever he actually meant to say to you.

Forgiveness, as we have established in part 1, can only occur between a creditor and a debtor, between the one harmed and the one who caused the harm. This is not a contingent relationship; it is part of the very meaning of forgiveness.

And yet Jesus forgave the sins of the paralyzed man in Capernaum and the woman in Simon's house, neither of whom had done him any harm.

Are we to conclude, therefore, that Jesus was speaking nonsense, like our stranger on the street?

God forbid, as Paul might put it. But then, what other explanation is possible?

Recognizing, at some level at least, this fundamental parameter of forgiveness, commentators in the past have sometimes elaborated on the biblical accounts in such a way as to make them conform to this conceptual necessity. The man and the woman, these apologists speculate, must have had some previous acquaintance with Jesus, and on those previous occasions, they must have done something to him that would qualify them for his forgiveness.

But surely this is grasping at straws. In the case of the paralyzed man, there is absolutely nothing in the text (or the parallel texts in Matthew and Luke) that would even suggest such prior acquaintance. Indeed, the account seems at pains to distance, so to say, Jesus from personal familiarity with the paralytic. It is the man's friends whose altruistic behavior sets the stage for his pronouncement, and his attention, up to the moment of his words of forgiveness, is focused on them, rather than the man himself.

And even in the case of the compromised woman, where it might be and has been speculated that her effusive display of affection towards Jesus indicates some prior familiarity with our Lord on her part, so that his pronouncement in Simon's presence was simply a reaffirmation of his forgiveness on that prior occasion, there is still absolutely nothing in reflective common sense that would suggest that the earlier acquaintance would have established an appropriate relationship for forgiveness.

Assuming her "sin" to have been sexual in nature, as most commentators are agreed, are we to imagine that her past sinful behavior had involved Jesus as a participant? Obviously not. So even if we suppose that her remarkably attentive behavior towards Jesus in Simon's house was an expression of continued gratitude for an earlier act of forgiveness, and that the words spoken in Luke's text were merely a repetition of the forgiveness accomplished on that previous occasion, that merely moves the impossibility to an earlier date. For how could Jesus have forgiven her *then*, having *then* not suffered personally from her wantonness?

So we are back at our dilemma. Neither the paralyzed man nor the woman of the street had, on this or any earlier occasion, done anything to harm Jesus personally. How then can he forgive them?

And yet he does; he forgives them both. And we are led thereby to a momentous truth, the truth that opens up the glorious reality of forgiveness as it exists, not only in the merely material universe, but in the universe created, maintained, governed, and loved by Almighty God, the divine Father of the divine Son, the divine Father of us all.

What is that truth?

Here is that truth: to sin against any of God's children is also to sin against God.

* * * * *

Our investigation of the concept of forgiveness has taught us that forgiveness can only be accomplished by the recipient of the harm caused by the errant behavior. Our analyses of the specific cases of the paralyzed man and the woman in Simon's house have convinced us that Jesus was not material party to their prior sinful behavior. And yet he forgives them.

There is no way of avoiding the conclusion that, therefore, their sinful behavior in the material realm of their lives must have harmed Jesus in the nonmaterial realm of his, the realm of the divine, the realm of God.

That is what logic teaches. Is there anything in Holy Scripture that provides corroboration of this conclusion?

The answer, of course, is that Scripture contains exactly that corroboration, as straightforward and unambiguous a revelation of divine reality as can be found anywhere in Christ's instruction. We find it in chapter 25 of Matthew's Gospel. Let me quote the entire parable.

> When the Son of Man comes in his glory, and all the angels with him, then he will sit on his glorious throne. Before him will be gathered all the nations, and he will separate people one from another as a shepherd separates the sheep from the goats. And he will place the sheep on his right, but the goats on the left.
>
> Then the King will say to those on his right, "Come, you who are blessed by my Father, inherit the kingdom prepared for you from the foundation of the world. For I was hungry and you gave me food, I was thirsty and you gave me drink, I was a stranger and you welcomed me, I was naked and you clothed me, I was sick and you visited me, I was in prison and you came to me."
>
> Then the righteous will answer him, saying, "Lord, when did we see you hungry and feed you, or thirsty and give you drink? And when did we see you a stranger and welcome you, or naked and clothe you? And when did we see you sick or in prison and visit you?"

> And the King will answer them, "Truly, I say to you, as you did it to one of the least of these my brothers, you did it to me." Then he will say to those on his left, "Depart from me, you cursed, into the eternal fire prepared for the devil and his angels. For I was hungry and you gave me no food, I was thirsty and you gave me no drink, I was a stranger and you did not welcome me, naked and you did not clothe me, sick and in prison and you did not visit me."
>
> Then they also will answer, saying, "Lord, when did we see you hungry or thirsty or a stranger or naked or sick or in prison, and did not minister to you?"
>
> Then he will answer them, saying, "Truly, I say to you, as you did not do it to one of the least of these, you did not do it to me." And these will go away into eternal punishment, but the righteous into eternal life. (Matt 25:31–46)

"As you did it to one of the least of these my brothers, you did it to me. . . . As you did not do it to one of the least of these, you did not do it to me." The scriptural attestation refers to an experienced *benefit* in the divine realm as well as an experienced harm. That is, of course, an extraordinarily significant fact as well, with profound implications for the Christian. But it is not our present concern to discuss those implications. Our present concern—the concern of this book—is to understand the role and importance of Christian *forgiveness* in divine creation, and a necessary stage in arriving at that understanding is to see how divine forgiveness of human misdeed is even possible, given what forgiveness in essence is: the acceptance of harm done to oneself. Our Lord in the parable above gives us explicit warrant for asserting that divine forgiveness resolves the same situation that human forgiveness does: a creditor-debtor relationship.

We have previously drawn attention to the commonplace situation in which a single harmful act may have multiple victims: my errant driving may damage my neighbor's fiancé's car as well as her own; the terrorist's bomb may injure a crowd of people; and so on.

Such examples are drawn from the merely material realm. But as Christians, we do not believe we live in a merely material realm. Ours is a realm that has a divine dimension in addition to the three (or more) dimensions that occupy the mathematical attention of those concerned with investigating the shape and nature of purely material reality.

And what our parable teaches us is that, in the material/spiritual creation we inhabit, our sinful behavior always has at least two victims, one (at least) in the material world, and another in the divine.

We are not told what the sins of the paralyzed man or the wanton woman had been; nor do we know the identities of their victims. But we do have it on divine authority that, whatever those sins were and whoever their recipients, corresponding harms were occasioned in heaven. And it is self-evident, therefore, that the forgiveness Jesus grants in their cases was for heavenly harm, the harm done to his own person, in his divinity.

At this juncture the reader will undoubtedly find questions arising in his or her mind as to the exact nature of the harm suffered by God. God is omnipotent, after all, and how can omnipotence experience harm?

We will address that question in chapter 6; but first, it will help us in our investigation to say a few words about the nature of the activity itself that occasions such harm, the activity that Scripture often refers to as *sin*. It is sins, after all, that Jesus forgives, not other sorts of harmful behavior.

5
Sin

In our discussion of human forgiveness in part 1, we established that such forgiveness can only meaningfully be extended in cases where someone believes himself—rightly or wrongly—to have suffered harm at the hands of someone else. At this point, it is important to make explicit something that has heretofore only been tacit in that discussion, and that further qualifies the context for such cases: not all nonfinancial harm caused by one individual to another is a suitable candidate for human forgiveness, but only such harm as results from what is perceived to be morally culpable behavior.

If during a friendly game of tennis, I twist my ankle in attempting to return your serve, the injury, while unfortunate, creates no occasion for my forgiveness. Why not? Because you have done nothing wrong; you have not morally wronged me in any meaningful sense. While I might on such an occasion use the language of forgiveness—"It's OK, I forgive you, you rascal!"—it would be understood by both of us that I was speaking ironically, or perhaps to comic effect. I would be feigning rather that registering moral aggrievement.

And similarly even for cases of more egregious harm. If I legally sell you a firearm, and you subsequently use the gun to shoot someone, the shooting victim cannot coherently forgive me, even though I was part of the causal chain of events that led to the shooting, any more than the victim could coherently forgive my parents for having given me birth.

Both stories could of course be elaborated in such a way as to make the forgiveness conceptually coherent. If I believe that you had previously and mischievously oiled the part of the court on which I was returning serve, I might then rationally blame you for my accident; or if I sold you the firearm, despite knowing you to be prone to criminal violence, the shooting victim might reasonably blame me, along with the shooter. Either incident might then at least offer a conceptually suitable occasion for forgiveness. But absent such elaborations, the harmful human activities described would simply offer no opportunities for forgiveness.

The point is that not all cases of experienced harm are suitable candidates for forgiveness, but only those in which the infliction of harm is believed by its recipient—whether correctly or not—to involve some element of moral culpability on the part of the person causing the harm. To put this another way, forgiveness in its extended uses beyond the realm of merely financial harm finds conceptual opportunity only in cases in which the recipient believes the harm to be morally blameworthy. Forgiveness and moral culpability are thus conceptually bound together; forgiveness is a potential resolution of perceived moral indebtedness.

Secular moral terminology does not provide us with a convenient catchall term for referring to any and all activities that include at least an element of moral grievance: perhaps *wrongdoing* comes closest. But traditional English religious terminology does provide us with such a term. That term is *sin*, and that is the term we will use in the remainder of this book.

But whatever term is used, the point remains that forgiveness, whether human or divine, is conceptually bound up with those behaviors in which the experienced harm is perceived by its recipient to contain at least an element of moral malfeasance.

It is not within the scope of our present investigation to discuss the various secular moral theories of what constitutes malfeasance or wrongdoing. Nor even is it within our purview to settle the hoary theological debate of whether sin—spiritual wrongdoing—simply amounts to disobedience to God's requirements, or whether those requirements arise from something independent of God's fiat: *Is behavior sinful because God forbids it, or does God forbid it because it is sinful?* as the issue is often framed.

Our concern is simply with the harm that results from sinful behavior and its forgiveness, whatever the resolution of that ancient conundrum. For our purposes, it will be sufficient if we can simply agree to the following generalization resulting from our earlier analyses: In divine forgiveness, God absorbs the counterpart harm to God caused by sinful harm inflicted on any of God's children by another of those children. When I sin against another of God's children—that is, against anyone—the counterpart vector of harm that extends into heaven creates the opportunity for divine forgiveness. It is the *sins* of the paralyzed man in Capernaum against his unnamed victims that Jesus forgives, not any of the other non-sinful, non-culpable human harms of which he may have been the source. As perceived moral culpability is conceptually bound with human forgiveness, so actual sinful culpability—given God's omniscience, there can be no cases of misperception—is conceptually bound with divine forgiveness.

And with that agreement in hand, we are now equipped to proceed to a discussion of the momentous issue postponed at the conclusion of the preceding chapter: the nature of the harm done to God by sinful human behavior.

6

The Nature of Divine Harm

WE ARE STEPPING NOW onto holy ground, and it is imperative that we do so with the proper perspective and the appropriate humility. Considering all of our human limitations along with the danger of hubris, when we venture to say anything at all about the nature of God, it must be with the prayer that nothing be said except what flows from the pious employment of that power of reflection which is itself God's gift. And so that is our prayer.

Our investigation of the concept of forgiveness has brought us to the conclusion that for God to forgive, God must be harmed. The author is well aware that theological disputants might at this point insist that we stop and deal with the general question of how the thought of harm is even compatible with the thought of God: the all-powerful, the eternal, the unchanging.

In response, the author must beg forbearance. Venturing off onto those deep theological seas would require a lengthy—perhaps interminable—detour, and we might thereon lose sight of our original destination: the province of Christian forgiveness. So in what follows, we will simply take it as assumed that the idea of God experiencing harm is not incoherent. Those who are dismayed by that assumption may wish to turn immediately to the chapter entitled "Speculative Theology" which concludes part 2, where we venture a few provisional reflections on the matter.

For the rest of us, we will simply for now take as warrant for our assumption that God can experience at least something analogous to human harm the fact that Jesus, on one occasion, wept, and on another, gave voice to his sorrow over the prospects for his beloved Jerusalem.

* * * * *

When a child is harmed, whether physically or emotionally, the harm experienced by the child's mother is obviously not identical to that experienced by the child, but neither typically does it even, so to say, mirror that harm. The mother neither feels the hand burned from touching the hot stove nor does she share the child's sudden disorientation and fear of the appliance. The child's painful experience is the cause of the mother's, but the two characteristically have nothing other than that material connection in common. Is there nonetheless a way of describing her harm which is both true and informative, yet independent of the endless variety of circumstance?

We must necessarily speak in general terms, because the specific nature of the mother's distress will vary according to her own personality, her unique relationship to her child, the nature and degree of the child's injury, and so on and so on. But do we have a way of describing, in general, the harm incurred by the mother, such that it will be true of virtually any mother's experience responsive to the suffering of her child?

Yes, we do. We may say in all cases—in all cases in which the original mother-child relationship is not in some way pathological—that the harm experienced by the mother is some variety of wounded parental love.

When a woman learns on the television news that a child in a neighboring community, a child unknown to her personally, has been injured in a car accident, she may react in many different ways, depending on her own personality. Those various reactions may range from emotional indifference, on one extreme, to quite acute emotional disturbance in someone of exceptional empathy.

But in no case, even when the symptomology might be similar, will they be instances of that distress that constitutes a mother's wounded love.

And just so, the harm done to divinity by harm done to any of us will always be an instance of wounded parental love.

Can we say anything more specific than that about the nature of the harm done to divinity by analogy to our human illustration? Can we compare it to a mother's anxiety, a mother's sense of helplessness or responsibility, a mother's heartbreak?

Perhaps we can, but we must postpone that discussion until later. For now, we will first seek corroboration for the analogy of parental love in the Christian understanding of divinity.

And such corroboration comes immediately from the most reliable of sources. The analogical figure that Jesus himself chose to refer to God and recommended to us was *father*.

And does our heavenly Father stand in relation to us in some analogy to the love of human parent? Indeed he does:

"For God so loved the world, that He gave his only begotten Son" (Matt 3:16).

And does our heavenly Father's parental love embrace all his children? He loves them all indeed:

> But God shows his love for us in that while we were still sinners, Christ died for us. (Rom 5:8)[1]

1. Although its author is a Christian universalist, it is not the project of this present work to deal with the soteriological implications of our heavenly Father's universal love for his children, in terms of their ultimate universal salvation. It is sufficient for our purposes here simply to request acknowledgment from the reader that God loves all his children, and that therefore the nature of the harm experienced by God on the occasion of harm to any of those children is informatively analogous on all such occasions to wounded parental love. It is the author's hope that even those who advocate for something less than universal reconciliation will nonetheless acknowledge the appropriateness of the analogy. Maintaining that God's parental love might be outweighed by some other elements of the divine nature—God's justice, for example—would still allow the wounding of that love even in its subordination to those other elements. And for our purposes of understanding divine forgiveness and its importance in the divine economy of salvation, that would still be sufficient. We will save the defense of universalism for another occasion.

So we will assume without further argument that harm incurred by any of God's children produces a corresponding harm—some divine analogy of wounded parental love—to God. And if we can proceed with that understanding, it now makes perfect sense how Jesus could forgive the sins of the paralytic in Capernaum and the wanton woman in the house of Simon the Pharisee.

Our earlier perplexity had been due to the fact that Jesus had clearly never suffered personally from the sinful behavior of either of these individuals, while our analysis of forgiveness has shown us that only the one harmed is in existential position to provide forgiveness to the source of that harm. The conclusion earlier forced upon us by these two premises is that Jesus cannot, could not, forgive those malefactors.

Given our discussion above, however, the resolution of the difficulty is straightforward: one of the two premises is false, viz., the premise that Jesus had not personally suffered from their behavior. While it is doubtless true that Jesus, in his temporal humanity, had not suffered at their hands, he had certainly done so in his divinity, as the eternal Son of God.

Understanding his forgiveness in that way enables us to make two additional points about the nature of the forgiveness Jesus extended to the paralytic and the serving woman.

The first is that the nature of the forgiveness offered them would be of a piece with forgiveness in general, as we have analyzed it earlier. God's forgiveness, like all forgiveness, will consist in absorbing the harm done to himself, neither asking nor expecting nor desiring anything further of the perpetrator of that harm. It means, at least in complete forgiveness, acting and feeling towards the perpetrator, exactly as if the harm had never been incurred. It means, in effect, forgetting his or her sin.

In discussing the difficulties of complete human forgiveness in chapter 2, we cited Jeremiah's great characterization of divine forgiveness, but it is worth quoting it again here:

> But this is the covenant that I will make with the house of Israel after those days, declares the LORD: I will put my law within them, and I will write it on their hearts. And

> I will be their God, and they shall be my people. And no longer shall each one teach his neighbor and each his brother, saying, "Know the LORD," for they shall all know me, from the least of them to the greatest, declares the LORD. For I will forgive their iniquity, and I will remember their sin no more. (Jer 31:33–34)

And second, this understanding of the relationship of divine parental love to human suffering caused by sin also stands in perfect accord with one of the constraints of forgiveness we noted in our earlier discussion. When a single action creates multiple harms, it thereby creates multiple opportunities for forgiveness, and those opportunities are essentially distinct from one another. When my driving mishap damages my neighbor's car and her car in consequence damages her fiancé's car, there are now two opportunities for forgiveness—hers and her fiancé's—and these two have no essential connection with each other. My neighbor's forgiveness may or may not be matched by her fiancé's, but there is no conceptual connection between the two.

Similarly, divine forgiveness of a particular individual's sin has no conceptual connection with the forgiveness of that particular behavior on the part of its human victim.

When Jesus forgave the sins of the paralyzed man, he did not thereby relieve that man's obligations to those he had sinned against, whoever they were. The human debt remains, even when the divine obligation has been absorbed.

An instruction Jesus offers during the Sermon on the Mount lays emphasis on this conceptual independence:

> You have heard that it was said to those of old, "You shall not murder; and whoever murders will be liable to judgment." But I say to you that everyone who is angry with his brother will be liable to judgment; whoever insults his brother will be liable to the council; and whoever says, "You fool!" will be liable to the hell of fire.
>
> So if you are offering your gift at the altar and there remember that your brother has something against you, leave your gift there before the altar and go. First be

> reconciled to your brother, and then come and offer your gift.
>
> Come to terms quickly with your accuser while you are going with him to court, lest your accuser hand you over to the judge, and the judge to the guard, and you be put in prison. Truly, I say to you, you will never get out until you have paid the last penny. (Matt 5:21–26)

The instruction here is often interpreted as being about the necessity of you forgiving your human victim in order for you to be forgiven by God. But the concluding verses make it clear that cannot be the correct interpretation. The failure to be reconciled with your neighbor is represented in those verses as resulting in a judgment against you by the court. You must, therefore, have been the perpetrator of the original dispute: you are the one who owes your adversary, not vice versa. He is taking you to court; you are not taking him. Or in other words, you are in his debt, and the reconciliation must depend on his forgiveness of you, and not yours of him.

The central point of the illustration therefore is, not that divine forgiveness requires a precedent human forgiveness, but that they are two separate matters. Divine resolution does not *ipso facto* resolve human conflict: independently of how matters stand between you and God, figured here by your attendance to temple ministrations, your human relationships still require separate and independent interpersonal human resolution.

When Jesus forgave the sins of the paralyzed man, he did not thereby relieve the man of his human responsibilities for harm done to his anonymous victims. Suppose that harm included neglect of his children. Did the forgiveness Jesus provided the paralyzed father entail the healing of the children's emotional wounds? Of course not. The father still remains in his children's emotional debt, and any resolution of that situation—perhaps through the children's forgiveness of their father—remains a strictly human affair.

The elder brother in the great parable of the forgiveness of the prodigal son gives vivid figure to the same point. The father/God forgiving the prodigal/sinner leaves untouched and unresolved the human relationship between the two sons. The open-ended conclusion of the parable leaves us with the hope but not the assurance that the elder son will mirror their father and forgive his brother. Whether or not that happy event occurs, however, is a separate and entirely human transaction. Divine forgiveness, here as everywhere, remains a model for human forgiveness, not its replacement.

Scripture does of course contain several passages in which Jesus points to the importance (some would argue even the necessity) of divine forgiveness being preceded by human forgiveness. "Forgive us our debts as we have forgiven our debtors" is a central petition of our Lord's Prayer, and in commentary upon that petition, Jesus asks theoretically how we may expect to be forgiven if we have not done so ourselves, and there are other examples in Scripture of this same concern.

These are most certainly important passages to deal with, and we will do so in our chapter on the benefits of forgiveness. But it is worth noting at this point that the parable of the prodigal mentions nothing of the kind. The father in the parable, representing God, lays no such requirement on his wayward son. The prodigal is not depicted as having forgiven anyone for anything, and yet the father completely forgives him.

And we have it on Saint Paul's assurance that "God shows his love toward us, in that, while we were still sinners, Christ died for us" (Rom 5:8). Assuming unforgiveness to be one of those sins, the natural reading is that God's forgiveness through Christ is unconditional, requiring no corresponding or precedent work on our part, including no work of forgiveness. How then are we to understand those passages in which Christ does, indeed, seem to posit such a condition?

These are important matters, and we must not be hasty or glib in examining them. But we do not as yet have all the tools in hand to do them full justice; so for now, we ask the reader's forbearance until such time as we have those tools in hand. Once we do,

I believe we will be able to reconcile these passages to the reader's satisfaction. For now, we are still on a journey of understanding.

And to complete this stage on that journey, we will now, as we earlier promised the theologians in our readership, offer some admittedly speculative reflections on the nature of God. Specifically we will discuss the means by which God accomplishes divine forgiveness of the sins of his children, namely, through his Christ, our heavenly Messiah. Those who are wary of treading any farther onto such hallowed ground may, without loss to our central argument, proceed directly to part 3.

7

Speculative Theology

In beginning the preceding chapter on the nature of divine harm, we emphasized that we were there treading on holy ground, and that is also the proper and circumspect way to preface the remarks that follow. The studies that we in our age combine together under the general term "theology" the ancient Greek fathers divided into two distinct branches, *oikonomia* and *theologia*. The former, as its name suggests, refers to the plan by which God orders and rules his household; it includes the means whereby God ransoms from sin, and the distribution of the gifts and graces of the Spirit which form part of the divine domestic ordering. The latter directed itself to the contemplation of Christ's eternal being —his relation to God and God's Spirit in the realm of eternity. That latter is the holy ground upon which we again now venture, and we must again do so for obvious reasons with the utmost humility. What we are now about to say has as its warrant only that it follows from a sincere and pious employment of the God-given instrument of human rationality, and as its prayer only that the theological speculation it offers provides no offense to the source and substance of all truth.

* * * * *

The man, Jesus, accomplished divine forgiveness of sins. The man, Jesus, was incarnate divinity. Therefore, that which of divinity became incarnate in Jesus is that which accomplishes forgiveness in heaven. That is our argument, in a nutshell.

The considerations that led us to affirm the first premise are provided in chapter 4 of this book. Scripture reports examples of Jesus, as a man, exercising an authority available only to divinity, that of forgiving the harm occasioned in heaven by human sin.

The second premise simply formulates the central conviction of orthodox Christian faith, expressed most succinctly in the opening verses of John's Gospel: "In the beginning was the Word, and the Word was with God, and the Word was God" (John 1:1). And it is the received truth of that conviction that makes the first premise intelligible: *because* Jesus was divine as well as human, he was able both to experience and absorb divine harm.

The conclusion follows from the truth of those two premises, and we may rest in its truth, while making no further claim to understand the nature of God. Whether the nature of God be Trinitarian or unitarian or something else altogether of which religious speculation has not yet conceived, we may, I believe, postulate with the complacency of uncomplicated faith that the following must be true: that which of divinity became incarnate in Jesus is that which, as divinity, accomplishes forgiveness in the eternity of heaven.

We may put this another way. That which of God forgives human sin in eternity became flesh and dwelt among us, and, as a man, accomplished that same forgiveness. If we may, in addition, give the name of Christ to that which accomplishes forgiveness in heaven, then we may put the same point this way: Christ became flesh and dwelt among us, and accomplished Christ's work on earth.

We will now step even further into the theological hallowed ground, and with the same prayer.

Whatever God does flows inevitably from God's own perfect nature, and is in that sense necessary. That of God which forgives human sins—what we are calling Christ—must therefore do so necessarily, meaning that, without Christ, God could not forgive sins. To employ to a different purpose the imagery we have used from the beginning, Christ carries God's burden of forgiveness; Christ relieves God of its burden. But we remember what forgiveness is, the acceptance and absorption of harm, in this case the harm done to divine parental love. The heavenly status of Christ, therefore, its privileged position, is to relieve God's parental suffering in eternity.

One last point before we conclude this theological speculation. We do not know what "time" means when used in reference to God, and *a fortiori* what it means for something to be the case "in eternity." These and their related locutions are phrases of the human vocabulary derived from the human experience, and applicable to spiritual reality only by a sort of blind fling into a darkness beyond human ken. We must refrain from thinking that we are flinging light into that darkness by using such terms. To say that God exists "outside of time" or that the things of heaven are "timeless" or anything else along those lines is equally futile in advancing human understanding into the realm of the divine. Our aim must never be to encompass God by human reflection, but always rather to trust in God's condescension to our honest attempts to find guidance in our human reality using only the tools available to that situation. We have the assurance of our inspired human record that Jesus forgave people their sins at certain times in human history, as humans reckon time and history. We have the assurance of faith that Christ's forgiveness is accomplished in the divine counterparts of time and history. More than that we cannot say, nor should we.

But if we may grant only that much, then I think we may proceed to an understanding of the nature and importance of Christian forgiveness, both in the life of the individual Christian, and in God's project of reconciling creation to himself. So let us now at last proceed to that investigation.

Part 3

Authority, Privilege, Responsibility, Benefit

8

The Christian Authority

We come at long last to the central concern of this book, which is to understand the nature and significance of Christian forgiveness, that is to say, of the practice of forgiveness by Christians.

When Jesus walked the earth, he was the only one who could forgive the sins committed against God; he was the only one who could absorb the divine harm resulting from the sinful behavior of people towards one another. As we have seen, that was why, as Christ incarnate, he could forgive the sins of the paralytic in Capernaum and the woman in Simon's house. He was simply manifesting as a man the same authority he had always exercised as the heavenly Christ, and his authority, in that regard, was unique to him.

And then something changed.

The sixteenth chapter of Matthew's Gospel records an account of an event that is sometimes referred to as the *hinge* of Jesus' earthly ministry. Having brought his disciples to the region of Caesarea Philippi, Jesus confronts them with the question of his own identity, and Peter, either speaking from his own private revelation or perhaps as the spokesman for the others, provides the hinge response:

> You are the Christ, the son of the living God. (Matt 16:16)

It is not our present intention to explore the magnificence and manifold meaning of Peter's words and of Jesus' response to them. Suffice it for now to say that Jesus welcomes that recognition, and does not dispute its truth. And from that moment on, his ministry moves into its concluding phase. That is why the moment is called the *hinge*.

But for our purposes, the important teaching that comes immediately after that recognition is what matters. The very first thing Jesus does after Peter becomes the first to acknowledge our Lord's true reality is to confer on his disciple a special authority. What is that authority? Here is the passage in full:

> And Jesus answered him, "Blessed are you, Simon Bar-Jonah! For flesh and blood has not revealed this to you, but my Father who is in heaven. And I tell you, you are Peter, and on this rock I will build my church, and the gates of hell shall not prevail against it. I will give you the keys of the kingdom of heaven, and whatever you bind on earth shall be bound in heaven, and whatever you loose on earth shall be loosed in heaven." Then he strictly charged the disciples to tell no one that he was the Christ. (Matt 16:17–21)

The authority given Peter, an authority before this moment belonging only to Jesus himself, is to act with respect to sinful behavior on heaven's behalf: to bind and loose in heaven.

Matthew's account gives us several examples of Jesus delegating divine authority to his followers. He gives them authority to preach on his behalf, sharing the same divine message of his own proclamation: "And proclaim as you go, saying, 'The kingdom of heaven is at hand'" (Matt 10:7). He shares with them his own divine authority over spiritual and physical affliction, even over death: "Heal the sick, raise the dead, cleanse lepers, cast out demons" (Matt 10:8). He authorizes them to render God's judgment of approval or disapproval on those who are receptive or otherwise to the gospel good news:

> And whatever town or village you enter, find out who is worthy in it and stay there until you depart. As you enter

> the house, greet it. And if the house is worthy, let your peace come upon it, but if it is not worthy, let your peace return to you. And if anyone will not receive you or listen to your words, shake off the dust from your feet when you leave that house or town. Truly, I say to you, it will be more bearable on the day of judgment for the land of Sodom and Gomorrah than for that town. (Matt 10:11–15)

But it is the authority to forgive that marks the turning point of Christ's ministry with respect to his followers, a fact emphasized by Jesus immediately before he confers it on Peter:

> And I tell you, you are Peter, and on this rock I will build my church, and the gates of hell shall not prevail against it. I will give you the keys of the kingdom of heaven, and whatever you bind on earth shall be bound in heaven, and whatever you loose on earth shall be loosed in heaven. (Matt 16:18–19)

Commentators and theologians wrangle, of course, over the extent of Peter's authority, and whether it is exclusive to him. But the authority to loose and bind in heaven, following immediately as it does upon mention of the keys to the kingdom of heaven, surely implies that that authority, if not exhaustive of, is central both to the stewardship of heaven's prerogatives (the keys) and to the project of building up the earthly church (the rock).

To loose and bind in heaven. What more natural interpretation of these images could there be than that of providing or withholding heaven's forgiveness? Those you forgive on earth are forgiven in heaven; those you refuse to forgive remain in heaven's debt.

And of course, those are exactly the terms Jesus uses in John's Gospel, in addition to extending the authority to all his other disciples. On the very day of his resurrection, after breathing his Holy Spirit upon them, Jesus immediately gives them the same authority earlier conferred upon Peter, this time explicitly in terms of sharing heaven's power to forgive:

> Jesus said to them again, "Peace be with you. As the Father has sent me, even so I am sending you." And when he had said this, he breathed on them and said to them,

> "Receive the Holy Spirit. If you forgive the sins of any, they are forgiven them; if you withhold forgiveness from any, it is withheld." (John 20:21–23)

Before moving on to discuss this authority in more detail, let us pause a moment to consider the true wonder of what we are learning here.

As we have established in our earlier discussion of forgiveness in general, all people, Christian or otherwise, have the opportunity to forgive another for the harm suffered at that person's hands, which is to say, to absorb the harm, to accept its full burden. That is simply what it means to forgive. Difficult it may be to do so, sometimes very difficult indeed, especially to absorb it fully, to forgive completely. But the possibility is there for everyone, at least as a spiritual destination.

But on the witness of Scripture the follower of Christ is given an additional opportunity, an additional project. It is the project of rising above the realm of merely human accomplishment, and participating in the divine. The authority Jesus confers on those who receive his glorified Spirit is unlike and far greater than any available to the rest of humanity, no matter how elevated their worldly status might be. It is the authority—and the privilege, and the responsibility—of acting as a divine representative of Almighty God in the matter of forgiveness.

Even the least of these Christians, one might almost say, is in this regard greater than all those who had gone before.

* * * * *

Having taken that moment to wonder at God's gracious condescension to the followers of Christ in granting them the authority to forgive on heaven's behalf, we must immediately make clear that such authority does have a limitation that Christ's own authority does not.

When Jesus forgave the paralyzed man, he was forgiving the sins of a stranger. Jesus was forgiving the man for harm he caused to others, not to Jesus himself.

And similarly for the immoral woman in Luke's account. Jesus was, again, forgiving her for harm she had done to others, not to Jesus.

As we have discovered, Jesus in these two separate events was acting as God incarnate. The harm these two had done had in fact also been done to Jesus as God incarnate. That is why Jesus could forgive them, even though he had not humanly participated in whatever their sinful behavior had been.

But it goes without saying that Christians are not God incarnate. Our authority does not extend to the forgiveness of strangers. How could it, since we by definition have not been harmed by them?

The magnitude of the human privilege of extending divine forgiveness is staggering, but its scope is limited. It is limited to the forgiveness of those who have done us harm.

The Christian privilege of forgiving sins is not innate to them because of who they are, as it was innate to Christ; but is rather an authority vested in them by virtue of something they have done, namely, accepted Jesus as the Christ, and as their Lord and Savior. In the spiritual nature of things, a Christian does not suffer from the behavior of strangers, as Jesus did. Christians, like non-Christians, suffer only from the harm done to themselves, and can forgive only that harm. We Christians are the ambassadors of God's forgiveness for the harms done to us, not the harms strangers do to each other.[1]

1. Readers of this investigation, especially those of the Catholic faith, will certainly have found points of comparison in it to the long-standing practice of granting the authority of absolution and the remission of sin to the priesthood of the Catholic faith, particularly since both that practice and our argument make fundamental appeal to the same biblical texts.

While it is not within the scope of this treatise to resolve the differences between our application of those passages and their application in Catholic tradition, it will be useful here to point out what those differences are, with the hope that future investigation and debate will at least have a shared focus.

The differences are twofold. The first is that we affirm that the authority to offer divine forgiveness of sins is conferred in those passages upon all Christians, and not only, as was asserted in the Council of Trent, to the Apostles, and to their lawful successors, where "lawful successors" includes only the Catholic

Having noted the limitation of its scope, we conclude this chapter by reemphasizing how nonetheless extraordinary this authority is that Christ has bestowed on his followers. Christians are allowed to enter into God's own activity, to participate on the spiritual plane in the ongoing evolution of God's plan of salvation. The authority to forgive on heaven's behalf is a privilege unique to Christians among all of God's children.

But having said that, we must now become clear about the special and solemn nature of that privilege.

At least in olden times, as children mature within a household, they gradually begin to assume some of the responsibilities previously borne by their parents and perhaps their older siblings. They begin to participate in the functioning of the household, not simply as carefree children, but as chore-sharing members. They begin to help bear the burden of running the house.

When Christians practice forgiveness, they are exercising the privileged burden of helping to manage the household of heaven.

---

priesthood.

The second is that, whereas the Catholic tradition claims for the priest the authority to forgive behaviors from which the priest has received no personal harm, our position is that Christian forgiveness can coherently only be extended where personal harm has been experienced.

It will be seen, therefore, that in our way of thinking, Christian forgiveness is in one sense more extensive, and in another more restrictive, than is postulated in the traditional Catholic practice of priestly absolution. It is more extensive in that it is an authority extended to all Christians, rather than to a particular credentialed class. And it is more restrictive in that it may be extended only by those Christians who have suffered sinful personal harm, and only to those who have been the sinful perpetrators of that harm.

9

The Christian Privilege

Speaking in general terms, to be privileged in some regard means one of two things. It means to be separated from others either in terms of having a special status or of having a special accomplishment that they do not have. Let us consider these possibilities in turn.

To be privileged by one's status or position may result from many different sorts of factors. Some may simply be matters of happenstance, with no suggestion that the position results from special merit or effort on our part. Thus we often say things along the following lines: "I was privileged as a child to be introduced to the president of the United States." When used in this way, it means something virtually indistinguishable from "I was fortunate."

When we speak of a privileged social class or race, the term is often being used in this sense. The class or race into which we are born is determined by elements outside of our control, and yet, for better or worse, those social and racial statuses often carry with them special rewards and tend to elicit attitudes of special regard from those not so privileged. We may, perhaps, inveigh against the unfairness of this special social or racial status, but that is to object to its morality, not its reality. We may protest that such privilege is unearned, but that is to impugn its genesis, not its existence. As a child's privilege of meeting a president speaks merely to the fact of the encounter, not to its special circumstances, so also the social or political criticism of class privilege does not address the *meaning* of privilege, only its distribution. Even to argue that all social privilege should be eradicated would not be to alter its meaning, but rather to contend for its elimination. We might in the same way argue that all children should henceforward be denied access to the president; but that would not alter the privilege of such a meeting: it would only eliminate its opportunity.

The point is that privilege always implies a separation from others in some special regard, whatever the source or moral propriety of that separation. The citizens of the United States are privileged to vote in America's elections, not in those of France, and vice versa. Children who have met a president will always retain the privilege of having done so, even once all future presidents are limited to adult contact!

Or again, privilege often attaches to special accomplishment or appointment. A soccer player may be privileged to compete on behalf of the United States in world competition by virtue of her having earned a spot on the national team due to her athletic prowess; a man may be privileged to represent his country in the United Nations by virtue of having been rewarded for earlier service. Both may be said to have earned their respective privileges, and thereby differ in that respect from the cases discussed above. But the logic of privilege remains unaffected, even when the grounds for its possession are less fortuitous than the accidents of birth or circumstantial happenstance.

Having a privilege, whatever its source, means to be distinguished from others in regards to the consequences associated with that particular fundamental distinction, whether those consequences be akin to the bragging rights of the fortunate child or to the representative rights of the ambassador.

The Christian privilege is the authorization to accomplish divine forgiveness of sin. The question whether that privilege is more like that of a child privileged to have met a president or more like that of an athlete privileged to represent the United States at the Olympics is an age-old theological debate. There are various ways of phrasing the debate, all of which circle around the issue of whether becoming a Christian is a reward for our having done something or believed something, or whether it is entirely an unearned gift of grace. Intimidating terms like "predestination," "free will," and so on provide the vocabulary for such debate in academic circles. But our present concern does not require settling or even entering into such debate.

Nor need we enter the controversy of what being a Christian, a follower of Christ, actually means, whether it is a fixed and forever status or whether it may be forfeited; whether some degree of hypocrisy in its profession may be tolerated or not; whether there are gradations in its privilege, as there are gradations of rank in a military; and so on.

Our concern in the present investigation is simply the revealed connection between the privileged authority to accomplish divine forgiveness and being a Christian, whatever further investigation or revelation might determine concerning exactly what being a Christian amounts to, and whether or not its privilege is in some fashion or other *merited*. Our purpose for now is simply to move on to a clear understanding of what that privilege is, and we will accordingly set those hoary controversies aside, to be examined on another occasion.

* * * * *

The privileged authority conferred on followers of Christ—those imbued with his glorified Spirit since Pentecost—is to share in the divine forgiveness of sins, that is, the forgiveness of harm done to oneself by another's sinful behavior. But we must now recall what we established in part 1, that forgiveness, by definition, entails a cost: forgiveness, in fact, simply *is* that cost, assumed by the one who forgives. My neighbor assumes the financial cost of repairing her car, waiving all claim on me for monetary recompense. Similarly, if the harm is emotional rather that financial—the harm resulting from insulting her, say—her forgiveness consists in her waiving all expectation of me rectifying the situation, of her assuming with no demand for assuage the emotional harm caused by my behavior. In the case of perfect, complete forgiveness, she in effect forgets my insult.

The Christian authority to forgive is therefore the authority to accept *in Christ's stead* the correlative harm caused in the divine realm, the harm done to divine parental love, by sinful behavior in the human realm. And exactly as in the merely human realm, that forgiveness entails a cost. When Jesus forgave the sins of the paralytic, he waived all divine claim on the man; his forgiveness being perfect, he in effect forgot the man's sin. By absorbing without demand for recompense in any sense the harm done by that man to divine love, he restored the man's relationship to God to what it had been prior to the sinful behavior. That is the authority the Son of God has from God the Father. And it is that same authority that Christ bequeaths to his followers, to all Christians.

The question then arises naturally: Why would Christ bequeath that authority?

In the tenth chapter of his Gospel, Luke records how Jesus, having earlier sent out his twelve disciples to spread his message, now appoints seventy others to the same mission. The number seventy is not chosen arbitrarily, but is clearly intended to hearken back to Num 11:16–17, in which Moses recruits the same number to lighten his own burden:

> Then the LORD said to Moses, "Gather for me seventy men of the elders of Israel, whom you know to be the elders of the people and officers over them, and bring them to the tent of meeting, and let them take their stand there with you. And I will come down and talk with you there. And I will take some of the Spirit that is on you and put it on them, and they shall bear the burden of the people with you, so that you may not bear it yourself alone."

The delegation of authority described in Luke is most commonly understood to signify Jesus, so to say, extending his own reach to those to whom he could not personally minister, and most particularly, to those to whom he would not be able to minister after his own death. He is training a cadre of ambassadors, according to this interpretation, to extend his ministry, not only into the surrounding cities and towns, but also, and much more importantly, into the world's future.

But while that task of laying a foundation for his future church was unquestionably part of Jesus' earthly work, it was not the central rationale for Moses in selecting his seventy elders to share in his work: they were not chosen to extend his reach, either in space or into future generations. Why then were they chosen? The answer is given quite explicitly in the text: to "bear the burden of the people with you, so that you may not bear it yourself alone." Moses had never borne the burden of dealing with those outside of his immediate jurisdiction, not to mention those of the future. The burden he was seeking to lessen in appointing the seventy was the burden which he, Moses, was bearing at the time.

The symbolic significance for Jesus in choosing that particular number, seventy, therefore lay not—or at least, not only—in extending his future ministry, but rather in lightening its current burden, and by implication, its eternal burden as well. The seventy for Moses were coworkers, not ambassadors, either present or future, and surely that is the point Jesus is making through that symbolic number.

What then is the burden that Jesus is asking his followers to share?

In the realm of eternity, as we have already argued in our chapter on speculative theology, the Son of God accepted the burden of extending divine forgiveness to all of God the Father's rational creation, that is to say, of bearing the burden of absorbing the harm caused to divine parental love by the sinful actions of God's children. That is the burden Jesus authorizes and asks his followers to share.

To put the conclusion succinctly: that authority conferred on Christ from God is the same authority Christ Jesus in turn confers on his followers. And what is that authority? Given our understanding of what forgiveness is, the answer is now clear. It is the authority to suffer in Christ's stead. Or to express this conclusion in another way: the heavenly privilege accorded to and accepted by Christ is to absorb the divine cost of forgiveness on God's behalf;

and just so, the heavenly privilege accorded to and, hopefully, accepted by Christians is to absorb the divine cost of forgiveness on Christ's behalf. In the accomplishment of divine forgiveness, the Christian stands to Christ in the same relation that Christ himself does to God the Father.

The Christian privilege is the privilege of suffering in Christ's stead.

In the strictly material, human realm, having a privilege typically carries a positive attitudinal connotation. But even there, that is a contingent matter: the privilege of representing the United States in the United Nations' deliberations may be experienced as burdensome by the US ambassador; the privilege borne by the ambassador may be experienced in the way the privilege of Simon the Cyrene was when he was allowed the privilege of helping to bear Jesus' cross on the *Via Dolorosa*, as burdensome or perhaps even painful.

In fact, since it invokes in reality the very image we have used from the beginning of this book to represent forgiveness, Simon's assistance on that doleful avenue may provide the perfect illustration for the privilege allowed to all Christians of sharing the burden of the heavenly Christ, the burden of bearing the cost of divine forgiveness of human sin. The Cyrene took a weight, that of the cross, from Jesus' shoulders.

"That's not a privilege I would choose to acquire!" one might understandably exclaim. "Isn't Christianity a system of rewards and benefits?"

Well of course it is that, but it is more than that.

The question may be framed in this way: Are the followers of Christ, of any era, to be regarded merely as his material descendants or as his contemporary spiritual coworkers?

Should our image of the relationship between Christ and his followers be likened to that of a king who built a small castle on his land, and then on departing from this earthly life left his children with a grand vision for the property, now theirs, along with a set of instructions for its maintenance and growth and elaboration?

Or should our image incorporate the Christian belief that *our* divine king still lives, and that our work benefits not only his vision, but the king himself?

Although it is admittedly not a decisive argument, perhaps a homely image Jesus himself once used to describe the privilege he was offering to his followers will help incline the reader to the acceptance of the second of these as the better description of Christ's preferment. "Take my yoke upon you and learn from me," he counsels them in Matt 11:30. The Palestinian yoke was fashioned for two draft animals to work under, side by side in coordinated effort. The less experienced of the two animals would learn from the first how to labor most profitably, but all the while in doing so, it would be sharing and thereby lightening the burden of its more seasoned counterpart.

Is it sacrilege to regard our Christian labors as not only advancing Christ's work of spreading the kingdom to the ends of the earth, but also as benefiting him during its accomplishment? I think not. Children of a king, after all, may be expected to make the king's life less burdensome, at least once they come of age.

* * * * *

The authority that Jesus devolved upon his followers in the great investiture of Pentecost is the authority to forgive sins—that is the Christian authority. The exercise of that authority is the sharing of Christ's burden of forgiveness—that is the Christian privilege.

What remains to be discussed is the Christian responsibility to assume that authority and to exercise its privilege. That will be the subject of our next investigation.

10

The Christian Responsibility

The Christian authority is to offer divine forgiveness of sins. The Christian privilege is to share in the sufferings of Christ through our forgiveness. The next thing for us to discuss is the Christian responsibility for doing so, and we will begin by thinking about the role that human forgiveness in general plays in preparing souls to receive the good news of Jesus Christ, that is to say, in growing the kingdom of heaven on earth.

* * * * *

In many of his parables, Jesus imagistically communicates God's intention that his kingdom is to grow, so to say, from the ground up, rather than be imposed from the top down. Jesus' imagery is invariably that of organic increase, of seeds developing gradually over time, of leaven working its way through the dough. The temptations in the wilderness are all in various ways temptations to accomplish his ends through the simple and immediate exercise of fiat of the divine architect, rather than the laborious and seemingly inefficient and failure-prone efforts of human agency. God's revealed intention is to *bring forth* his kingdom by a laborious process from the raw material of his creation, to raise earth to heaven, rather than bring heaven down to earth.

The difficulties of that process are incarnated in the very life of Jesus. His birth in a stable manifests the poverty of the instrument God has chosen. The reaction of his own family at the outset of his instruction and the blindness of many to whom his good news was offered manifest the folly, the unreasonableness, of how that process must seem to practical, even sympathetic, human intelligence. The smallness of the gate and narrowness of the road speak to its difficulty, and Jesus often mentions the sacrifices and even the dangers of persecution it entails. Being one of his followers, from a purely worldly perspective, seems fraught with material hardship.

And in some eras and locations of Christian history, those admonitions were literally borne out, as they continue to be borne out in some parts of the world even to the present day. But for many other Christians they would seem to have application only in some extended or metaphorical sense. Relatively few of us in our age and situation are persecuted in any serious way for our Christian faith, and most of us lead comfortable lives from a material point of view.

One possibility, therefore, is to regard these warnings as applicable only to *some* of his followers, to his earliest converts certainly, and to those of later generations who find themselves in similarly oppressive social circumstances.

Another possibility is to regard them as posing a hypothetical requirement: that *all* Christians must be *willing* to endure such worldly hardships, whether or not they ever materialize.

Neither of these possibilities, however, reflects the universality of the individual responsibility that seems everywhere in the Gospel accounts to be Christ's instruction. Humility, mercy, purity are not enjoined on his followers selectively or hypothetically, but on them all, in all life's circumstances.

But there is another possibility, namely, that what is uniformly required of his followers is something that is inherently difficult for human accomplishment, but is nonetheless enjoined on them, in every place and every time.

In part 1, we discussed the difficulties of forgiveness, and we pointed out how the activity of forgiveness runs contrary to our ubiquitous human qualities of pride and vanity, violates our "higher" faculty of moral judgment, and often subjects us to the condescension and contempt of others. That is why full forgiveness—completely merciful and utterly anonymous—is so rare of occurrence.

And yet this is the very instrument, this frailest of reeds, that God has chosen to accomplish his purpose of spreading his own nature throughout his rational creation.

Why?

Because it is necessary.

* * * * *

Christianity is spread from person to person. It is not based on mob appeal or tribal conviction. It is, and can be, spread only through the individual acceptance of Jesus as Lord and Savior. That is the plain and simple meaning of John 3:16:

> For God so loved the world that He gave His only Son, that whoever believes in Him should not perish, but have eternal life.

The acceptance of Jesus as Savior occurs when and only when the individual has recognized the reality of the forgiveness of that individual by God. That is the gospel way. The principal resistance to that recognition is unfamiliarity with the human reality of forgiveness. Without familiarity with human forgiveness, the news of God's forgiveness remains, for most, simply a theory, a matter of doctrine, an acknowledgment of the intellect, not of the heart.

If you have lived all your life in the tropics, the reality of being cold must remain an abstraction. You can read books about the hardships of arctic exploration, but the conditions you are reading about will always remain an affair of the imagination—like a blind person hearing about colors—and never a lived reality, will never hearken to personal experience.

Until you have been forgiven, not just in the abstraction of religious doctrine or the contemplation of devotional reading or the pious acceptance of pulpit assurance, but in the lived reality of human experience, it also must remain something theoretical, something perhaps for your intellect to fit into a network of other concepts and doctrines. Your embrace will be that of a theologian, not that of a repentant sinner.

As someone who has never left the tropics, you might still be able to speak with learned authority about the history of arctic exploration, perhaps even make intelligent suggestions about appropriate equipment and prudent itineraries. But however great your expertise, you would still remain an "armchair" explorer.

Christianity spreads through individuals not just acknowledging but experiencing the reality of God's forgiveness. But that is extraordinarily unlikely to happen without first having experienced the reality of forgiveness in the ordinary sphere of human interaction. Human forgiveness effects the softening of the heart that is a prerequisite for receiving the good news, the word, of divine forgiveness. That softening is the preparation of the ground, the good earth into which the seed, when sown, can take root, and grow, and in time yield its own fruit.

That is the main reason why the offering of the gospel, the good news of divine forgiveness, is so often ineffective: because those to whom it is offered have not been softened by the reality of human forgiveness. The ground has not been prepared.

And that is why forgiveness, human forgiveness, is the key to the spread of the kingdom. It is not the key that opens the gate for oneself; it is the key that opens the gate for others. Without the preliminary work accomplished by human forgiveness—and we have seen how difficult that work may be—God's own forgiveness cannot take root in a human spirit.

And that is why, knowing the frailties of the human spirit, knowing how hard it is to forgive, Jesus groaned in the garden, and asked his Father whether there might not be another way.

* * * * *

We have discussed the power of human forgiveness: it is that which prepares the spirit to receive the good news of God's forgiveness through Jesus Christ. That power can of course also be exercised by non-Christians. The non-Christian as well as the Christian can accept the harm occasioned towards themselves by the sinful behavior of others, and the recipients of that forgiveness are thereby to some degree, at least, prepared to accept the good news of heaven's forgiveness through Christ, when it is preached to them. Christian conversion would be much rarer than it is if it could only be accomplished within Christendom!

What distinguishes Christian forgiveness from merely human forgiveness in the project of growing the kingdom is therefore not its power of preparing souls to receive the gospel. What distinguishes Christian forgiveness is that it is not only a power—it is a responsibility. By virtue of its authority and privilege, Christian forgiveness is also a duty.

Duties and responsibilities attach to people as an adjunct of their particular status. A nation's ambassador, by virtue of the special powers and privileges associated with the office, thereby acquires that office's responsibilities. We may say the responsibilities are the cost of that office. They are what the ambassador is duty bound to fulfill, in exchange for that status.

As we have seen, the special status of being a Christian involves both a special authority and a special privilege. The authority of the Christian is to forgive sins on heaven's behalf. The Christian privilege is to suffer in Christ's stead in the exercise of that authority. The office of the Christian, thus authorized and privileged, has the adjunctive responsibility of exercising its privileged authority to forgive.

For the non-Christian, while an act of forgiveness may reflect well upon his character, it is not something that is required of him by God. He does not occupy the requisite office. In Paul's image, he is not (yet!) part of the body of Christ; in an old and rougher image, he is not part of the army of God. A private citizen may well arm himself and fly overseas to combat the enemies of his country, but he is not obligated by his status to do so until and unless he has enlisted in his country's military.

* * * * *

This is a hard truth for many Christians to accept: Christianity is the narrow way because it entails not just special status and privilege, but special duty. And as we have now seen, that special duty is perhaps the hardest of all for human accomplishment: the duty to forgive.

Nothing we have said here implies or asserts that Christians will, any more than non-Christians, always forgive, or even that they will try to do so with any greater assiduity. We are only saying that Christians, unlike those, have a divine responsibility to do so. They may shirk their duty, but only because they have a duty to shirk.

Nor is to imply that those who shirk their duty thereby forfeit their status as Christians. We are not—far from it—perfect, even as our Father in heaven is perfect. There has only been one perfect Christian, only one whose forgiveness is unfailing and always complete, and his forgiveness extends even to our failures as Christians to forgive. It is not forgiving that makes us Christians, any more than swimming makes us a fish. It is forgiving that makes us obedient Christians, that manifests Christ's own glorified Spirit at work in our human lives.[1]

1. The project of this work is to clarify what Christian forgiveness is. A separate but equally important project would be to clarify the conditions under which offering it to someone who has done us harm is, from the Christian point of view, appropriate, or even mandated. This would involve considering the question of whether the appropriateness of Christian forgiveness presupposes or requires contrition on the part of the one who has inflicted the harm, that is, whether it is a *carte blanche* requirement, or whether its responsible proferment requires at least some apprehension of contrition or (to use the traditional Christian term) *repentance* on the part of its potential recipient. To grant that forgiveness is a Christian responsibility implies that its exercise be engaged in responsibly, and the extraordinarily interesting question of what that entails must remain the subject for another occasion.

But having thus received that blessed assurance, we may now point out that the practice of forgiveness by Christians certainly does bring with it wondrous and divine personal benefits. As we will now proceed to discover, fulfilling the duty to forgive is a comfortable yoke for Christians to bear, because it opens the door to all the blessings of heaven.

11

The Christian Benefit

IF YOU PERUSE THE BOOKS in the Christianity section of your local bookstore—assuming you still have a local bookstore—you will likely find several having to do with forgiveness. If you read any of those books, what you will invariably find is that they consist mainly of success stories about the remarkable emotional and psychological benefits that have accrued to individuals once they have forgiven someone. The person they forgive will invariably be someone of great biographical significance to them, whose behavior has occasioned in them long-standing feelings of anger or resentment, feelings they have harbored over time to the great detriment of their spiritual and even material lives. In these often poignant stories, the act of forgiveness, in whatever it consists, is experienced as a cleansing liberation, perhaps even something akin to a rebirth into a new and better life.

These are uplifting accounts, and they do indisputably illustrate a reality about human nature, that the actions we associate with acts of forgiveness do often result in changes in the forgiver's emotional life and attitudinal perspective, changes described by those who forgive in terms analogous to those they might use to describe physical recovery from a lingering illness or a debilitating injury.

And this is certainly a human reality about acts of forgiveness and their relation to the human spirit, a reality that psychotherapists as well as pastors would be wise to incorporate into their attempts to help those under their care to cope with and even overcome many sorts of pathologies rooted in perceived ill-treatment or neglect.

These accounts, however, humanly gratifying as they might be, tend to neglect the dimension of forgiveness which lies at its very heart, and which was the primary focus of part 1 of this book, namely, that true forgiveness, in its essence, is the assumption of an emotional and psychological burden: it is the acceptance, the assumption, of the damage done to oneself, with all that implies, and the deliberate attempt to return the relationship of the forgiver to the forgiven to what it had been prior to the harm. It is an act of the will, and while it may well have consequent emotional benefits, it also may not. As a practice of courageous resistance to tyranny *may* be experienced as self-affirming or in some other way emotionally rewarding, it also may not be experienced in any such welcome fashion; but in all cases, it entails the often considerable costs, spiritual and even material, of offering and maintaining that resistance. And so also with the act or practice of forgiveness, as indeed with all acts or practices of the virtuous will. An act or practice of forgiveness may be experienced as liberating or burdensome, depending on the other elements of the forgiver's spiritual makeup, but its attempt and accomplishment are independent of the nature of its emotional consequences.

But as we near the conclusion of our investigation, there is another and even more important point to make about the accounts of forgiveness we might find in our bookstore: they admirably illustrate the potential benefits of human forgiveness in general, but not the special and divinely guaranteed spiritual benefits of Christian forgiveness in particular.

Christians have a unique authority, a unique privilege, and a unique responsibility to forgive. But as we shall now proceed to see, their forgiveness also has a unique benefit.

* * * * *

In the middle of Matthew's version of the Lord's Prayer, we hear Jesus linking the petition for our own forgiveness to the forgiveness we offer others, and the gloss for that instruction immediately supplied by Matthew records Jesus saying this:

> For if you forgive others their trespasses, your heavenly Father will also forgive you. But if you do not forgive others their trespasses, neither will your Father forgive your trespasses. (Matt 6:14–15)

One interpretation of this instruction might have it that the great gift of salvation is contingent upon—or must wait upon—some act of forgiveness on our part. But such a simplistic and literal reading would run contrary to the entire gospel of grace, the good news that God's salvation has been accomplished without condition for all by the redemptive work of Christ. Ours is a religion of faith, not works. There is nothing we must *do* to acquire salvation, not even forgive others. We do not *earn* salvation; we accept it.

This great gospel truth is represented perhaps nowhere more clearly than in the mighty forgiveness parable of the prodigal son, whose wealth we tapped once earlier in chapter 6. Having squandered his resources, the younger son in the parable returns in embarrassed shame, and receives his father's embrace—his father's forgiveness—without having done anything to earn it, certainly without first having forgiven anyone himself. That is in fact the whole point of the parable, at least as it pertains to the younger son. The father's forgiveness is a free and unconditional gift of the father's grace, proceeding from the father's heart rather than the son's merit. The father's relationship with his son has been restored to what it had been prior to the son's sin, along with all the benefits of being a member of the household. To use our image of complete forgiveness, the father has, in effect, forgotten the transgression.

Given this understanding of the parable, we may therefore now understand the instruction of our Lord's special prayer, and his own gloss on its central petition. While the full meaning of our Lord's words must surely, this side of heaven, lie beyond our human understanding, we may say at least this much with confidence: the entire panoply of the graces associated with God's forgiveness of us is available only to those who have cultivated the quality of forgiveness within themselves. Salvation understood as the rescue from damnation is not the product of that cultivation; but salvation, in the sense of fully receiving and enjoying the fruits of Christ's indwelling Spirit, most certainly is.

Up to this point, we have emphasized that forgiveness is typically burdensome, and for good reason: because it is the accepting of someone else's burden. For a Christian, that burden is in a sense multiplied, because it entails not only bearing the burden of human suffering, but bearing some portion of the burden of God's suffering. That is the yoke of which we have spoken earlier, the yoke that Christ invites us to share with him.

But Christ also adds that his yoke is comfortable; it lies easily on those who choose to shoulder it alongside him.

What he is referring to are the spiritual fruits, the divine benefits, of Christian forgiveness.

* * * * *

Paul gives a list of such fruits in Galatians. Whether he was offering this as an exhaustive list is unknowable, but what matters for our purposes is that they are all qualities of spirit: love, joy, peace, patience, kindness, goodness, faithfulness.

It is noteworthy that the quality of being of a forgiving nature is not mentioned among those fruits, even though, as we have seen, its empowerment is the very first endowment granted to his followers by Christ, and its exercise, with the burdens that accompany it, is the chief responsibility that receiving and accepting that endowment entails.

The reason it is not mentioned is because it exists at a more fundamental level than they do. It is, in fact, their precondition.

* * * * *

We are all familiar with the old bromide that if you give a man a fish, you will be feeding him for a day, but if you give him a fishing pole, you will be feeding him for a lifetime. The general principle the adage illustrates is pretty straightforward, isn't it? Some gifts are foundational for other gifts.

And this general principle has applications throughout every aspect of our lives. The gift of self-discipline is foundational for the benefits accruing to artistic mastery; the gifts of certain sorts of personality are foundational for the benefits of friendship; the gift of pragmatic intelligence is foundational for the benefits for material achievement.

And at an even deeper level, the gifts of sight and hearing are foundational to our experiences of many kinds of beauty, the gift of mobility to the enjoyment of many sorts of adventure and play, the gift of health to the enjoyment of much of what the world has to offer.

When we start thinking about gifts in that way, it should soon occur to us that there is one gift that is foundational, not just to certain others, but to all the others. And that of course would be the gift of life. Without life itself, there can be no growth or development or enjoyment at all. It is the prerequisite for everything else. It is the soil out of which everything must grow.

Forgiveness of others, for the Christian, is the foundation of the new life, the new life from above. It is not a requirement for admission into the household of God; but it is the foundation for the enjoyment of all that heaven has to offer. The fruits of divine forgiveness are available to those, and only to those, who have opened themselves as conduits for spreading God's own nature—suffering love, forgiveness—throughout God's creation. That is the meaning of Jesus' gloss on his own special prayer.

In the great parable of the unforgiving servant, we find a perfect illustration of this dynamic of forgiveness. Let us read it in its entirety:

> Therefore the kingdom of heaven may be compared to a king who wished to settle accounts with his servants. When he began to settle, one was brought to him who

> owed him ten thousand talents. And since he could not pay, his master ordered him to be sold, with his wife and children and all that he had, and payment to be made.
>
> So the servant fell on his knees, imploring him, "Have patience with me, and I will pay you everything." And out of pity for him, the master of that servant released him and forgave him the debt.
>
> But when that same servant went out, he found one of his fellow servants who owed him a hundred denarii, and seizing him, he began to choke him, saying, "Pay what you owe." So his fellow servant fell down and pleaded with him, "Have patience with me, and I will pay you." He refused and went and put him in prison until he should pay the debt.
>
> When his fellow servants saw what had taken place, they were greatly distressed, and they went and reported to their master all that had taken place. Then his master summoned him and said to him, "You wicked servant! I forgave you all that debt because you pleaded with me. And should not you have had mercy on your fellow servant, as I had mercy on you?"
>
> And in anger his master delivered him to the jailers, until he should pay all his debt. So also my heavenly Father will do to every one of you, if you do not forgive your brother from your heart. (Matt 18:21–35)

The ruler forgives the servant's extraordinary debt, but the servant refuses to extend that forgiveness into his own world. The ruler accepts the harm the servant has inflicted, but the servant refuses to do the same on behalf of his own debtor. And as a result, the servant is banished from God's presence, figuratively removed from receiving any further blessings that might attach to his membership in the ruler's household.

In the seafaring era of ages past, when message flags were hoisted on the mast to communicate with a distant observer, the messaging ship might fire a gun to emphasize the message's importance. Jesus often does something like that in his parables, concluding with a dramatic note to emphasize the importance of what he's teaching. In this parable, the ruler imprisons and tortures the servant for the latter's failure to forgive. Aside from running contrary to the good news, this is almost comically not God's way; but it does lend weight to the parable's message: that God's continued and evolving and ever-greater beneficence is withheld from those who refuse to conform their nature to the most fundamental element of God's own.

* * * * *

The spiritual qualities that Paul mentions—love, joy, peace, and so on—are certainly qualities that might figure in their human versions in the lives of those who are not Christian. But there is this difference: as they emerge and grow in a Christian, they have their root in the divine presence of Christ's indwelling Spirit, rather than in the accidents of our biology or circumstances of life. "Not as the world gives, I give unto you," Jesus says of his peace (John 14:27), the peace that passes all understanding. *His* joy is the joy that he would have us experience, not the fleeting worldly emotion we normally associate with the word.

And similarly for all the other qualities, when they are fruits of the Christian spirit. Their roots receive nourishment from that uncanny soil comprised of the divine mingled with the material, which is the new life of the born-again Christian. The heavenly fruits that are maturing within us may not be recognizable, even to ourselves, as those named by our human vocabulary. Christian humility, as many have profoundly noted, does not mean thinking less of oneself; it means thinking of oneself less. It names something that may not even lie within our human apprehension.

But we may say this much, on divine authority: the qualities so rooted, so grounded, are those which will render us suitable to continue to grow and mature in the environment of heaven. We Christians are in this world, but not wholly of it. Our love, joy, peace, patience, kindness, goodness, faithfulness are the imperishable fruits of heaven, and as Paul puts it, the perishable cannot inherit the imperishable.

Such is the benefit, to imperishable Christians, of forgiveness.

Part 4

How To Forgive

12

Practical Advice

We have now come to the end of our investigation of Christian forgiveness. We now know of its special authority, its unique privilege, its weighty responsibility, and its divine benefit.

We will conclude by saying a few words about a topic that has been latent in everything that has gone before. In the concluding verse of the parable of the unforgiving servant that we examined in the last chapter, Jesus makes reference to what he calls *forgiveness from the heart*, an apparent qualification that he mentions nowhere else in his various instructions about forgiveness.

Our discussion in the last chapter makes it clear that the divine consequences of Christian forgiveness are spiritual fruits, so that Jesus must be understood as saying here that the maturity and quality of those fruits is related to the considerations we advanced in chapter 1, and often returned to in our subsequent discussions, concerning how forgiveness can be more or less complete. Forgiveness in its fundamental sense is simply an activity, but in its more extensive and important applications, it incorporates conditions of the interior life of the forgiver. In these applications, to use the image we have often relied on, complete forgiveness consists in the forgiver, in effect, forgetting the sin. To put it another way, in simple financial forgiveness, forgiveness is either/or; in forgiveness of divine import, it lies upon a scale.

It is those cases and that scale that Jesus is clearly referencing when he speaks of forgiveness from the heart. The instruction to the Christian is that the ideal towards which he or she must strive, in forgiving, is one in which the interior life is, so to say, *aligned* with the public activities that communicate the forgiveness. In the ideal, there is no interior discord with the public expression, no regret, no hesitancy, indeed, no memory. As all of God's activities flow perfectly and inevitably from his own nature, and in so doing perfectly make manifest that nature, so also should Christian forgiveness, ideally, perfectly manifest the Christian's personal spiritual economy. Ideally, it should be as effortless, and as unconscious, as breathing.

And therein lies the problem of how to forgive, that is, of how to align our own spiritual nature with the activity of forgiving, or more generally, with the practice of forgiveness. How do we become creatures, not just of a forgiving practice, but of a forgiving nature?

* * * * *

As we did at the outset of our investigations, let us begin with some everyday examples.

How does a woman improve her cardiovascular condition? By regularly going to the gym and exercising on a treadmill. She cannot improve her fitness level simply by willing it to be so, but she can improve that level by willfully and conscientiously *doing* something. The internal improvement is accomplished incrementally and over time by her disciplined commitment to a certain pattern of outward behavior.

Or how does one lose weight? By altering one's eating habits, by choosing better food and consuming them in smaller amounts.

How does one get to Carnegie Hall? Practice, practice, practice, as the old joke instructs us.

In these simple and homely cases, the primary internal changes resulting from external behavior are purely physiological. But those who have engaged in these endeavors will often notice an accompanying change of attitude. As her fitness level improves, the time spent on the treadmill by our health-conscious walker is no longer experienced as drudgery, put rather as a pleasure. She enjoys the experience of her muscles in motion, and her previous attitude towards "those exercise nuts" begins to evolve. She prides herself on her disciplined commitment. She may even find herself making new friends with similar interests at the gym!

And similarly for our dieter. As his body begins to feel tighter and lighter, his self-confidence gradually returns. His outlook is no longer complicated by conscious or unconscious feelings of self-disappointment and self-criticism; his attention is freed to focus outward rather than inward; his interests are engaged by the world around him and the fresh opportunities it offers to his enhanced capabilities.

And our pianist, as her fingers grow more and more adept, as her hands and eyes and ears become more coordinated to a single purpose—creating music—so almost certainly will there be corresponding emotional and attitudinal changes: too many and too varied to list.

In these material and everyday examples, the point is that emotions and attitudes, even if not subject to immediate willful transformation, nonetheless can and often do evolve in response to our willful determination, to our deliberate behavior. In a word, the virtuous will is an achievement, often hard-won.

A good fairy tale, like a good parable, may sometimes communicate a human reality more effectively than a volume of abstractions. So let us conclude with a fairy tale.

THE MASK

There was once a king who ruled his subjects through terror and intimidation. His cruelty was so deeply ingrained in his nature that his very face was frozen into a terrible rictus of disdainful pride that instilled fear and dismay in everyone he met. But he didn't care, because those were exactly the emotions he wished to inspire.

But there came a time when from a distance he saw the beautiful princess of a neighboring kingdom, and for the first time in his life, he felt incomplete. He inquired, and learned that the princess was as lovely of character as she was of appearance. He longed to make her acquaintance and court her, but he knew that his terrible face would frighten her, and he would never have the chance of winning her love.

As his only resort, he sought out a local witch, and ordered her to fashion him a magic mask that would hide his true face, and instead show one of benevolence. When he tried the mask on, he could barely recognize himself in the mirror. Instead of arrogance, the mask showed an expression of humility; instead of cruelty, the mask showed kindness; instead of avarice, the mask showed generosity. When he smirked with gloating delight at the deceptiveness of the mask, the mirror showed back a gentle look of calm reassurance.

With confidence in the mask, he arranged to make the acquaintance of the beautiful princess.

The courtship took root, but the king quickly realized that in order for it to flourish, his behavior would have to support the illusion of the mask. Gritting his teeth—a friendly smile, through the mask!—he began playing the part of the benevolent ruler. And over time, he played the part well. The laws of his land came to manifest justice instead of tyranny. His people, at first wary, gradually turned to him for help and understanding. Neighboring kingdoms, once exploited, now found in him a cooperative ally. Most of all, perhaps, a feeling of general goodwill and peace spread over his country.

At long last, the king proposed marriage, and the princess accepted. But on the eve of their wedding, the king, moved by a strange urging of conscience that he had never before experienced, confessed to the princess what he had done, that ever since their first acquaintance he had been wearing a magical mask that disguised his true appearance. Before they could marry, he needed to show her his true face.

"Of course," she said. "But do not worry. I love your heart, whatever your face. Let me remove the mask."

> *And when she had done so, she studied him for a moment, and then said, with a quizzical smile, "My darling, you look exactly the same as the first day we met."*

And so we return to forgiveness. As we have noted many times now, forgiveness can be more or less complete, and full forgiveness—meaning the complete restoration of the emotional economy of the forgiver towards the forgiven—is a rare and noteworthy accomplishment.

But this divine ideal of complete forgetfulness, while perhaps not often attainable in this earthly coil, may still remain our guiding star, the destination that shapes our Christian efforts and directs our Christian journey. The old adage has it that we must never allow the perfect to be the enemy of the good, and we may find encouragement in the assurance that God will never require more of us than what is humanly possible.

And what is humanly possible?

Practice, practice, practice.

THE END

www.ingramcontent.com/pod-product-compliance
Lightning Source LLC
LaVergne TN
LVHW020649100826
845148LV00012B/2394

* 9 7 9 8 3 8 5 2 7 5 1 3 7 *